THE U.S. NAVAL INSTITUTE ON

THE PANAMA CANAL

U.S. NAVAL INSTITUTE
Chronicles

For nearly a century and a half since a group of concerned naval officers gathered to provide a forum for the exchange of constructive ideas, the U.S. Naval Institute has been a unique source of information relevant to the nation's sea services. Through the open forum provided by *Proceedings* and *Naval History* magazines, Naval Institute Press (the book-publishing arm of the institute), a robust Oral History program, and more recent immersion in various cyber activities (including the *Naval Institute Blog* and *Naval Institute News*), USNI has built a vast assemblage of intellectual content that has long supported the Navy, Marine Corps, and Coast Guard as well as the nation as a whole.

Recognizing the potential value of this exceptional collection, USNI has embarked on a number of new platforms to reintroduce readers to significant portions of this virtual treasure trove. The U.S. Naval Institute Chronicles series focuses on the relevance of history by resurrecting appropriate selections that are built around various themes, such as battles, personalities, and service components. Available in both paper and eBook versions, these carefully selected volumes help readers navigate through this intellectual labyrinth by providing some of the best contributions that have provided unique perspectives and helped shape naval thinking over the many decades since the institute's founding in 1873.

THE U.S. NAVAL INSTITUTE ON

THE PANAMA CANAL

THOMAS J. CUTLER
SERIES EDITOR

Naval Institute Press
Annapolis, Maryland

Naval Institute Press
291 Wood Road
Annapolis, MD 21402

Library of Congress Cataloging-in-Publication Data
Names: Cutler, Thomas J., 1947– editor of compilation. | United States Naval
    Institute, issuing body.
Title: The U.S. Naval Institute on the Panama Canal / Thomas J. Cutler.
Description: Annapolis, Maryland : Naval Institute Press, [2016] | Series: U.S.
    Naval Institute chronicles | Includes index.
Identifiers: LCCN 2016021519 | ISBN 9781682470442 (alk. paper) |
    ISBN 9781682470459 (mobi)
Subjects: LCSH: Panama Canal (Panama)—History. | Panama Canal
    (Panama)—Design and construction. | Panama Canal (Panama)—
    Strategic aspects.
Classification: LCC F1569.C2 U68 2016 | DDC 972.87/5—dc23
    LC record available at https://lccn.loc.gov/2016021519

♾ Print editions meet the requirements of ANSI/NISO z39.48–1992
(Permanence of Paper).
Printed in the United States of America.

24 23 22 21 20 19 18 17 16   9 8 7 6 5 4 3 2 1
First printing

CONTENTS

EDITOR'S NOTE

BECAUSE THIS BOOK is an anthology, containing documents from different time periods, the selections included here are subject to varying styles and conventions. Other variables are introduced by the evolving nature of the Naval Institute's publication practices. For those reasons, certain editorial decisions were required in order to avoid introducing confusion or inconsistencies and to expedite the process of assembling these sometimes disparate pieces.

Gender
Most jarring of the differences that readers will encounter are likely those associated with gender. A number of the included selections were written when the armed forces were primarily a male domain and so adhere to purely masculine references. I have chosen to leave the original language intact in these documents for the sake of authenticity and to avoid the complications that can arise when trying to make anachronistic adjustments. So readers are asked to "translate" (converting the ubiquitous "he" to "he or she" and "his" to "her or his" as required) and, while doing so, to celebrate the progress that we have made in these matters in more recent times.

Author "Biographies"

Another problem arises when considering biographical information of the various authors whose works make up this special collection. Some of the selections included in this anthology were originally accompanied by biographical information about their authors. Others were not. Those "biographies" that do exist have been included. They pertain to the time the article was written and may vary in terms of length and depth, some amounting to a single sentence pertaining to the author's current duty station, others consisting of several paragraphs that cover the author's career.

Ranks

I have retained the ranks of the authors *at the time of their publication*. As noted above, some of the authors wrote early in their careers, and the sagacity of their earlier contributions says much about the individuals, about the significance of the Naval Institute's forum, and about the importance of writing to the naval services—something that is sometimes underappreciated.

Other Anomalies

Readers may detect some inconsistencies in editorial style, reflecting staff changes at the Naval Institute, evolving practices in publishing itself, and various other factors not always identifiable. Some of the selections will include citational support, others will not. Authors sometimes coined their own words and occasionally violated traditional style conventions. *Bottom line:* with the exception of the removal of some extraneous materials (such as section numbers from book excerpts) and the conversion to a consistent font and overall design, these articles and excerpts appear as they originally did when first published.

ACKNOWLEDGMENTS

THIS PROJECT would not be possible without the dedication and remarkable industry of Denis Clift, the Naval Institute's vice president for planning and operations and president emeritus of the National Intelligence University. This former naval officer, who served in the administrations of eleven successive U.S. presidents and was once editor in chief of *Proceedings* magazine, bridged the gap between paper and electronics by single-handedly reviewing the massive body of the Naval Institute's intellectual content to find many of the treasures included in this anthology.

A great deal is also owed to Mary Ripley, Janis Jorgensen, Rebecca Smith, Judy Heise, Debbie Smith, Elaine Davy, and Heather Lancaster who devoted many hours and much talent to the digitization project that is at the heart of these anthologies.

Introduction

WITH THE PANAMA CANAL currently undergoing a major expansion, it is appropriate and enlightening to look back to the early days of this remarkable and somewhat presumptuous project. With its substantial maritime impact, it is not surprising that the canal was the subject of much thought-provoking dialogue in the Naval Institute's unique forum. Indeed many articles appeared in *Proceedings* magazine during the years that the canal was being built, and in the years following it has remained a subject of interest.

Details of its construction were of great interest as this truly amazing project took shape, and early writers capitalized on that aspect. One article by R. E. Bakenhus, a Navy civil engineer, appearing in 1913, goes into amazing detail about the history and construction of the canal. Because it is so detailed, it is nearly 28,000 words in length and had to be abridged in order to appear in this collection. But even after editorial surgery, there remains a healthy corpus of exposition.

Undaunted by the French failure to dig a canal connecting the Atlantic and Pacific Oceans during the 1880s, the United States took on this rather daunting project in 1904. Having solved some of the problems that had deterred the French—such as mosquito-borne diseases and danger-ous landslides—American engineers, doctors, and a host of other talented and determined people were able to complete the project by August 1914—coinciding with the outbreak of World War I.

The commercial importance of this undertaking was obvious, but as the canal became reality, the potential strategic significance was also not lost on naval and military planners. In the same year (1890) that he pub-lished his landmark treatise on maritime strategy—*The Influence of Sea Power*—Alfred Thayer Mahan published an article in which he claimed "the piercing of the isthmus is nothing but a disaster to the United States, in the present state of her military and naval preparation." Mahan was obviously making a ploy for a larger, more potent fleet, but his remark makes clear that there was significant strategic significance to the forth-coming canal, a contention that was to be echoed many times in the pages of *Proceedings* before during and after the construction of the canal.

Of particular interest is an article that appeared in 1914, written by Dr. F. Zadow, a German academic from the University of Greifswald. Not only is this piece notable as coming from a nation that would soon be at war with much of the Western world—including the United States—but the *translator* of this article was an up-and-coming Ameri-can naval officer by the name of Ernest J. King. There is a certain irony in the words offered by this German contributor who notes that the building of this canal will result in the "extraordinary strengthening of the strategic position of the United States, and of the maritime power thereby created," and predicts that "sooner or later there must come, as nearly as human judgment can predict, a decisive conflict in the Pacific." It is unlikely that the translating Commander King had any inkling that he would someday lead the struggle that would indeed come to pass, as the United States and Japan fought the greatest sea war in history in just a few decades. It is also probable that this German author would have been surprised to know that his nation would twice be at war with the United States in the years to come—and would twice be defeated.

Other articles appeared in the years following covering different aspects of the canal and its impact on world trade and strategic brinkmanship. Among the topics broached was the possibility for a second canal, notably addressed by then–Lieutenant Commander P. V. H. Weems, a frequent contributor to *Proceedings* who is remembered today for his contributions to the science of navigation. In the hallmark tradition of the Naval Institute as an open forum, A. W. Hinds, another frequent contributor, weighed in with his own views in the very next edition.

Thirty years later, Captain R. S. Fahle resurrected some of the concerns of Weems and Hinds when he discussed the limitations of the canal in terms of modern mobile warfare and the role of the aircraft carrier.

Another ten years brought another article—this one from Naval War College professor August Miller—warning of the canal's limitations and the need for feasible remedies.

More treatises followed in the decades to come, and the final article in this collection declares that "the Panama Canal makes two military ships out of one" and advocates the modernization necessary to provide the "absolutely thrilling sight" of "our largest carriers transit[ing] the Panama Canal."

Technological wonder, strategic game changer, and commercial benefactor, the Panama Canal has had an almost immeasurable impact on human history. These pages capture some of that impact, recounting the canal's glorious past, acknowledging the debates engendered by its existence, and showcasing some of the prognostications that have emerged and proliferated ever since its emergence onto the world scene over a century ago.

1 "Bunau-Varilla, Protagonist of Panama"

Captain George J. B. Fisher, USA

U.S. Naval Institute *Proceedings*
(September 1933): 1313–22

AS OUR SHIP PUSHES steadily across the Isthmus of Panama, we are constantly enveloped by an atmosphere of achievement. It makes itself felt as we rise through the locks of Miraflores and Pedro Miguel. In navigating the Gaillard Cut, there is the sense of sheer accomplishment. And the 85-foot drop at Gatun never fails to impart a thrill at what man hath wrought.

Here is tangible fulfillment. The dreams, the sweat, the blood of a fast-receding generation are all congealed into the masonry of the locks. The determination of our fathers is monumented for all time by breakwaters, dams, and now invisible excavations. The Stars and Stripes that float over it all bespeak creation just as proudly as they proclaim possession.

Yet we should never have had it except for the invincible will of a single Frenchman, Philippe Bunau-Varilla. Were it not for this resolute and single-purposed son of France, world traffic would today follow the Nicaraguan route from the Atlantic to the Pacific. It may yet, for that matter; but today Nicaragua remains a possibility while Panama is a reality. And behind all we have accomplished at Panama there hovers the shadow of Bunau-Varilla who so insistently pointed the way.

The dominant passion of Bunau-Varilla's life was that the canal at Panama should be created. To this he dedicated himself under De Lesseps. But when in time the French effort collapsed, there emerged from the debris the lone, erect pillar of this one Frenchman's determination. While all others fled, he stood steadfast. The creation of the canal now became to him a spiritual issue—nothing less than a vindication of French engineering genius. Nothing stopped this indefatigable engineer in the pursuit of his purpose. Discouragement, calumny, obstinacy, inertia, opposition, all melted in time before the intensity of his will. The impact of his personality on American thought came eventually to rival in his particular sphere that of Lafayette or De Grasse in theirs. The story of how he converted one antagonistic nation and disrupted another makes up a little-known romance of American history.

Bunau-Varilla first went to Panama in 1884, as a youth of twenty-five. A year before he had graduated from the Ecole des Ponts et Chaussées, but already, at the école polytechnique, he had fallen under the spell of the elder De Lesseps. So he sailed for America, imbued with the same patriotic fervor that carried so many young Frenchmen to their deaths under the banners of the Universal Interoceanic Canal Company. But the youthful Bunau-Varilla was not destined to fall a victim to yellow fever. Instead, he lived and thrived on the isthmus. Placed first in charge of the engineering works of Culebra and the Pacific slope, within six months he had command of two-thirds of the construction then under way.

We seldom give the French enough credit for what they accomplished at Panama. Not only did they pioneer; they had actually carried the project well on the road to completion when with the end in sight the battle was lost—not in Panama but in Paris. It was French politics coupled with indifferent financing that destroyed the confidence of the French peasant in his investment in Panama. The monarchists, anxious to discredit the republic, cried, "See what scandalous waste democracy had led you into!" The republicans in turn retorted, "Watch how democracy can punish inefficiency in high places!" When the smoke finally cleared away, Jean Homme had again hidden his hoard and the hundred-odd millions necessary to carry the canal to completion were not to be found. Confidence, on which the undertaking entirely depended, had vanished.

Finally, by 1893, even Bunau-Varilla was forced to admit that so far as France was concerned Panama was dead. Able resuscitator though he was, his every effort to reanimate the canal with French enthusiasm had failed. So he turned his face abroad. Not to the United States, however. The attempt to interest this country in the Panama plan came only as a final resort. Bunau-Varilla first took his ideas to Russia.

The Dual Entente between France and Russia had been signalized by Alexander's reception of the French fleet at Kronstadt in 1891. The alliance was cemented by a military concord between the general staffs of the two countries during the summer of 1892. Said Bunau-Varilla, "Why not energize this new defensive alliance with a peaceful undertaking which will bind the two nations together in a profitable economic enterprise?"

This proposition he laid before De Witte at St. Petersburg. The plan was for the Russian and French governments jointly to guarantee 3 per cent return on approximately $140,000,000 needed to complete the work of the French canal company. We know now that there was at least no engineering obstacle to the success of this scheme. The czar's government was willing and promised Bunau-Varilla a favorable reception of such proposals from Paris. But here again the project was wrecked by French politics.

The original concession granted De Lesseps by Colombia was due to expire in 1894. Its renewal was dependent upon active resumption of excavation. The prospect of reviving Panama as a joint Franco-Russian enterprise was therefore warmly received by the French cabinet. But then, unexpectedly, the receiver of the bankrupt canal company obtained an extension of the concession from Bogota. The need for immediate action ceased to be urgent. The politicians postponed; Carnot was assassinated;

a new cabinet inimical to Panama came into office; and Bunau-Varilla looked elsewhere for help to complete the waterway which he forever refused to desert.

Next he sought to interest British capitalists. In Egypt, on the occasion of the thirtieth anniversary of the opening of the Suez Canal, he laid the project before an audience of English shipping magnates. Bunau-Varilla said,

> Here is a waterway whose eventual success will surpass even that of Suez. Conceived by the same great engineer, it now suffers from nothing more than the same lack of confidence which Mr. Gladstone entertained toward the Suez just a few years ago. Why not make France's loss Britain's gain, take over the uncompleted works and give the world an all-British canal across the Isthmus of Panama?

To this proposition Chamberlain, the British Colonial Minister, lent an attentive ear. He promised it serious consideration as soon as the Boer War could be disposed of. But by that time the Panama project had entered its final stage. The United States had become interested.

For half a century and more this country had with varying degrees of earnestness considered a Central American canal. Each of our wars quickened interest in shorter transport between the Atlantic and the Pacific. After the War with Mexico came the era of exploration. Following the Civil War, we definitely decided where the waterway should be built. The Spanish-American War ushered in the era of execution. But the definite decision of 1876—that the canal should be constructed across Nicaragua—was altered on the very eve of execution. Congress in the Spooner bill of 1902 chose the much maligned "French" route via Panama in preference to the long-favored "American" canal across Nicaragua. Behind this sudden and complete reversal of American Policy may be traced the intensive efforts of M. Philippe Bunau-Varilla.

The first overtures from Panama to the American government came as a letter, dated November 18, 1898, addressed to the President, and offering to sell to the United States all concessions, property, and other belongings of the French on the isthmus. In this offer Bunau-Varilla had no part. He was in Paris at the time, having ended his official relations with the works upon the failure of the old company. But his interest in Panama was unceasing and the offer provided a cue which he was quick to accept. In aggressively supporting the lukewarm proposal of the canal company, he could not help but see he was acting on a forlorn hope.

Repeated surveys of the isthmus had been made by leading American engineers whose reports invariably favored Nicaragua. Grant's interoceanic canal commission reported in 1876 that the Nicaragua route . . . "possesses greater advantages and offers fewer difficulties from engineering, commercial, and economic points of view than any of the other routes." This became the American doctrine at the international scientific congress assembled by De Lesseps at Paris in 1879 to place the approval of science on his Panama project. Admiral Walker's technical commission of 1897 had returned the same verdict. Public sentiment in the United States was definitely committed at the turn of the century against the Panama route. We were resolved to build a canal and to construct it across Nicaragua, which would have spelled the complete doom of the French ditches at Panama. So Bunau-Varilla now saw, if he was to realize his cherished dream of seeing the French plan vindicated, that there was no alternative but to sell the De Lesseps idea to the United States.

This enthusiastic Frenchman cherished innumerable friendships in all parts of the world. His enemies he grouped in a single category— those who opposed the Panama waterway. Most men who came within reach of his persuasive eloquence were quickly transformed first into friends of Bunau-Varilla and then into advocates of the Panama route. It was the fate of John Bigelow to become exposed to the Bunau-Varilla influence as early as 1885. Then, in the heyday of French activity, when 12,000 to 14,000 men were actively engaged on the isthmus, various influential chambers of commerce were invited to send representatives to Panama to examine the accomplishments of the French company. The New York Chamber of Commerce sent Mr. Bigelow who came, who saw, and who departed a firm friend of the young French engineer and a devoted advocate of Panama. Eighteen years later this friendship bore fruit. Bigelow was then the octogenarian sage of the McKinley administration. The Secretary of State, John Hay, had been his legation secretary in Paris in the years following the Civil War. To him Bigelow earnestly recommended that the forthcoming presidential message to Congress refrain from a definite commitment to the Nicaraguan route. Thus the way was paved for the looming "Battle of the Routes."

Mr. Bigelow went to Washington personally to urge on the government a reconsideration of the entire proposition. Nevertheless, in January, 1899, the Senate passed a bill authorizing the construction of a Nicaraguan canal. In February it went to the House where it met opposition as to form but not as to substance. The House was overwhelmingly in favor of a Nicaraguan canal, yet objected to the administrative features of the Morgan bill. The close of the session approached without compromise on either side when suddenly a new resolution was introduced. This provided for a new isthmian canal commission to review the entire ground and report on the relative advantages of Nicaragua and Panama. John Bigelow's winter in Washington had not been in vain.

Here another Bunau-Varilla friendship comes into play in the romantic drama of the contending routes. This time a naval officer enters the plot, Lieutenant Commander Asher Baker. This officer was attached for duty with the Paris Universal Exposition and while in Paris came under the spell of our French proponent of Panama. It happened that Baker had intimate personal relations with Speaker Reed and with Chairman Cannon of the House Ways and Means Committee. So aroused was Commander Baker with Bunau-Varilla's exposition of the advantages of the Panama route that he prevailed on these two influential Congressmen at least to see that the cause of Panama received a hearing. But Commander

Baker's more important contribution came in one of a series of remarkable coincidences that accompanied Bunau-Varilla's efforts to bring the conception of De Lesseps to final fruition.

One evening during the summer of 1900 our French engineer set out to visit a friend in the Latin Quarter. The friend was not at home. This seemingly inconsequential absence of a Parisian householder started a chain of events that resulted in the creation of a new republic in the Western Hemisphere. Faced with an idle evening, Bunau-Varilla decided to dine out and very casually selected the Restaurant Fayot. He found the dining-room deserted except for a single table occupied by three Americans. One was Commander Baker who immediately insisted that the Frenchman meet his companions. They were H. T. Proctor and W. W. Taylor, two Cincinnati manufacturers and capitalists. Oddly enough, Bunau-Varilla did not mention canals during the ensuing meal. But he promptly reciprocated the hospitality of his new-found friends with a luncheon, when he lost no time in setting forth the advantages to the United States of advancing the French works to completion. The Americans were impressed. "In the United States we know nothing of all this," they said. "Well, I will go and tell it to your people when you give me the signal," replied Bunau-Varilla. There the matter rested. It was just one of innumerable lines that Bunau-Varilla had out, all baited with the possibilities of Panama. But on this line he soon had a first-class strike.

In December there came a cable requesting him to visit and lecture to the Cincinnati Commercial Club on the relative advantages of Panama and Nicaragua as canal routes. It was the opening wedge. Not a large opening, to be sure, and Bunau-Varilla had little in the way of leverage against the dead weight of a nation's opposition to his views. There were the stalwart Bigelow, the naval officer Baker, and his two Cincinnati friends; but there was also his own crusading enthusiasm. These were enough. Eighteen months after Bunau-Varilla sailed for New York, in January, 1901, the tide of public opinion had turned and the die was cast in favor of Panama.

On the voyage to America, Bunau-Varilla occupied himself with his favorite diversion of creating friends for Panama. Years earlier, while traveling across Germany, a chance acquaintance paved his way to De Witte and the Russian cabinet. So this time a Catholic prelate, succumbing to Bunau-Varilla's statistics and eloquence, pointed him to Colonel Myron T. Herrick of Cleveland. From Herrick the trail led to Marcus A. Hanna, whose eventual conversion to the cause of Panama brought Bunau-Varilla very close to the attainment of his dreams.

In Cincinnati the French evangelist was received cordially, but with the sympathy accorded an advocate of a lost cause. His welcome thinly veiled ironic skepticism. Yet an opportunity to present his conception of truth was all he sought. His presentation of the possibilities of Panama so impressed an audience of business men that a few days later Bunau-Varilla was called to lecture on his favorite topic before the Cincinnati Society of Civil Engineers.

From Cincinnati Bunau-Varilla proceeded to Cleveland, carrying his campaign to the hearthstone of the McKinley administration. Then in Boston, Chicago, and finally in New York, he addressed select audiences of manufacturers, engineers, and economists. Next he published a pamphlet setting forth in print the charts and statistics and all the striking arguments he had presented from the lecture platform. While the mails were carrying this message to a wide circle of influential Americans, Bunau-Varilla sat in his New York hotel and balanced accounts. His first few weeks in a new and strange country had brought him many valuable contacts and, he was sure, some progress toward his goal. They had also brought a fresh realization of the tremendous handicap he must overcome if the cause of Panama was finally to triumph. Congress, he saw, was ready to support the construction of an isthmian waterway, but the Senate was committed to Nicaragua while the House was decidedly hostile to Panama. It was the national legislature that must be converted.

At the White House Bunau-Varilla called, in company with Charles G. Dawes. But he did not tarry long with McKinley. Instinctively he concentrated his efforts toward Hanna. Finally, the junior Senator from Ohio saw the light, even became an apostle. He said,

Mr. Bunau-Varilla, you have convinced me. Today I grasp clearly the whole question. . . . I am an old mining operator. If two mines are offered me, I prefer the one which I know to be good and which is said to be bad to the one which I know to be bad and which is said to be good. As a Senator of the United States, I must adhere to the same principles. . . . Naturally, it will be necessary that what you say should be ratified by men like Morison, Burr, or Ernst. If, as you assert, they think as you do, I shall go over on your side.

It was very evident at this time that a favorable report from Admiral Walker's isthmian canal commission was an essential prelude to any serious consideration of the Panama route by Congress. Morison, Burr, and Colonel Ernst were the only members of this commission who had not served on the Nicaraguan commission of 1897. All three had already come under Bunau-Varilla's persuasive oratory. As a subcommittee designated to study the Panama route, they had gone to Paris to examine the archives of the old French company. Here Bunau-Varilla waylaid them, and they left France in a frame of mind which justified the report to Senator Hanna that they would cast their weight toward Panama.

But the isthmian canal commission was unable to obtain from the French holding company a clear-cut proposal for the sale of its property. There was some difficulty with Colombia too, since the original concession forbade the sale of French rights. Yet it was the inertia of the representatives of the French owners that served effectively to dampen whatever enthusiasm Bunau-Varilla had been able to work up among his friends on the canal commission. As a result the commission reported to Congress, on November 16, 1901, just as had all preceding canal investigators, that Nicaragua presented the only practicable route for an American waterway.

This would have remained the last word on Panama had any but a very extraordinary man been so determined on realizing the De Lesseps idea. But the adverse report of the canal commission does not appear to have even discouraged the intrepid Bunau-Varilla. Here was just another obstacle to be surmounted. He promptly used his influence with the Parisian daily *Le Matin* to have the president of the French canal company dismissed and new officers who would talk business appointed. He then hurried back to Paris to prevail on the directors of the company to sell out to the United States. A flat forty million, he told them, would probably turn the trick. . . . Within a week after Bunau-Varilla reached Paris, Senator Hanna announced in Washington that the Senate canal committee was willing to reconsider the Panama route if the French rights could be bought for this precise amount. Attacked thus on two flanks, the French directors surrendered. Then, for the first time, the tide commenced to turn. A definite sale price having been agreed upon, the isthmian canal commission revised its findings and on January 18, 1902, recommended the Panama route to Congress.

Meanwhile McKinley had been assassinated and Roosevelt came into office. With the passing of McKinley, Hanna's power waned. Roosevelt perfectly understood the wide popular sentiment in favor of Nicaragua and as late as 1905 stated that he would never have accepted Panama except for congressional pressure. But Bunau-Varilla had builded well on his first visit to America. Hanna remained in the Senate and, once fortified with the technical opinion of the isthmian canal commission, he seriously took up the fight for Panama.

Still it is unlikely that the Senate would have wavered from its allegiance to Nicaragua except for an unusually fortuitous circumstance. Three weeks before the opening of the senatorial debate on the canal issue Mont Pelée erupted. The attendant destruction of the town of St. Pierre left with the public a vivid fear of the dangers of volcanoes. Within a month and while volcanic activity continued at Martinique came word of the eruption of Momotombo in Nicaragua. This was plain confirmation of Bunau-Varilla's repeated assertions that Nicaragua was subject to seismic disturbances which would endanger any canal built in that country. For the first time the Senate's faith in Nicaragua was shaken. But a telegraphic inquiry was sent to Managua, in reply to which the President of Nicaragua cabled, denying any volcanic eruptions in that country. This heartened the senatorial friends of Nicaragua, who declared that the reported eruption of Momotombo was merely a scheme of Bunau-Varilla to stampede the United States into accepting Panama. The pro-Nicaragua Senators went a step further and announced that Nicaragua was not even volcanic. Here they overplayed their hands and gave Bunau-Varilla the opportunity for his most brilliant coup. He promptly scoured the stamp dealers of Washington and succeeded in buying ninety Nicaraguan one-centavo postage stamps. The copy of this issue which I have shows Momotombo prominently and most picturesquely erupting. One of these stamps Bunau-Varilla placed in the hands of every member of the Senate. "Here," he said, "is an official witness of the volcanic activity of Nicaragua."

Three days later the Senate voted. By a majority of eight, it passed the Spooner bill. But the House remained obdurate. It, too, had to be shown. There were no more Nicaraguan postage stamps to be found in Washington. So Bunau-Varilla took a train to New York where he collected some five hundred. Hurrying back to Washington, he distributed one with an appropriate legend to each Representative. The same evening the House delegates gave way to the Senate and accepted Panama as the route of the canal.

So the "Battle of the Routes" was won. On its editorial page the *New York Sun* briefed the struggle in two paragraphs:

The victory for Panama has been fairly won on the merits of the case, and there is now general acquiescence throughout the country.

Many persons, forces, influences, circumstances, and accidents have contributed to the fortunate result. If we were asked to catalog some of the principal factors, we should promptly mention President Roosevelt, Secretary Hay, the Hon. Marcus Alonzo Hanna, Senator Spooner's genius for doing the right thing at the right time, the monitory eruption of Momotombo, and last but not least, the former chief engineer of the French work on the isthmus, M. Philippe Bunau-Varilla, who throughout the negotiations has typified the good sense and good faith of the Paris shareholders and has likewise illustrated in his own person a sort of resourceful which some people are accustomed to regard as peculiarly American.

At this point it might seem that, with his victory won, M. Bunau-Varilla could have retired to France for a well-earned rest. He did sail forthwith, but in Paris he still kept his ear to the ground. It is fortunate that he did, for soon the Panama project was threatened with an entirely new danger. The Spooner bill accepted the Panama route with two provisions: (1) that clear title to the French works could be obtained and (2) that a satisfactory treaty with Colombia could be made; otherwise Nicaragua would be substituted. The first condition Bunau-Varilla had already provided for. The second condition was never met. Yet in the transfer of Principals Bunau-Varilla emerges as a statesman and plays a final, dominant role.

The Colombian government of 1903 had few honest reasons for failing to ratify the Hay-Harran treaty. Bunau-Varilla always contended that the same monarchial and reactionary influences that wrecked the Panama project in Paris worked to an identical end in Bogota. He sent several warning messages to Colombian politicians, pointing out that the isthmus would stage a duplicate of Cuba's recent revolt if they persisted in obstructing the completion of the waterway. Yet the Colombian Congress failed to ratify and by September of 1903 it became clear that the second condition of the Spooner bill could not be met.

On September 22, Bunau-Varilla arrived again in New York. This time he came on purely personal business, yet it was fortunate for the cause of Panama that he arrived when he did. He had been ashore only a few hours before he became entangled in a revolutionary plot that rivaled any dream of O. Henry or Richard Harding Davis. The central figure of the plot was Dr. Manuel Amador, erstwhile physician to the Panama Railroad, a prominent citizen, and later to be president of Panama.

Amador came to the United States on a secret mission for the Panama independence movement. He had been promised by parties in whose word he placed a childlike confidence that Washington would support the movement with funds and military force. But he was soon disillusioned. The government, he found, had not the slightest interest in the revolutionary project. On the same day Bunau-Varilla reached New York, Amador was despondently deliberating whether he should return defeated to Colón, or if he had not better assassinate the man who brought him to the United States on a fool's errand. Instead, he sought out Bunau-Varilla and through him found the straight road to independence. The Frenchman was able to supply what the Panaman lacked: energy, incisiveness, and wide contacts with men of affairs. His more or less fortuitous encounter with the revolutionary movement at this precise moment had a determining effect on subsequent history. As John Bigelow later remarked to him, "the world is more indebted to you than to any other person for giving a new republic to America."

It was clearly seen by the inhabitants of the isthmus that the inaction of a Congress sitting in the remote Andean highlands would spell their ruin. For half a century the province had lived and fattened on the transportation activities represented by the Panama Railroad. These would most certainly wither and die if the United States were obliged to desert Panama and build its interoceanic highway across Nicaragua. The isthmus would revert to primeval slumber and its inhabitants to primitive occupations. This grievance far surpassed those behind most Latin-American revolutions.

"Just what do you seek in America?" asked Bunau-Varilla.

"Arms, ships, and money," responded Amador. "Our people are brave and determined, but we must have $6,000,000 to carry through the revolt with any hope of success."

"Be patient," was Bunau-Varilla's advice. "In a few days I shall tell you what can be done."

There appeared just two possibilities of circumventing Colombia's refusal to assent to the building of the canal at Panama. One was for the American government itself to invoke the treaty of 1846, which guaranteed the United States the right of way via any means of transit across the isthmus—forcible coercion of Colombia. The second method was secession, the acquiring of new rights from a lesser state independent of Colombia.

Bunau-Varilla sought out his old friend William H. Burr, professor of technology at Columbia University, and through him met another member of the same faculty, J. Bassett Moore. From this authority on international law and close friend of Roosevelt, he obtained the opinion that the United States unquestionably had legal rights under the treaty of 1846. Yet the probability of enforcing them with the Nicaraguan alternative so easily at hand appeared so remote that to Bunau-Varilla the revolutionary method seemed the only solution.

The French engineer then went to Washington and through his friend, Francis B. Loomis, was presented to Roosevelt. At this interview the possibility of the secession of Panama was mentioned. Bunau-Varilla left the White House with two definite impressions: (1) that the President had not seriously considered the possibility of a revolution on the isthmus and (2) that he was inclined personally to follow the dictates of Congress and build the waterway across Panama if at all possible.

On the train back to New York, Bunau-Varilla analyzed his problem with engineering precision. What he had to decide was, how could a revolution at Panama succeed without the financial and military co-operation of the United States? He saw that the $6,000,000 demanded by Amador was not too much to provide the naval vessels necessary to prevent the maritime movement of troops from the Colombian mainland to Panama. He also understood that this sum was beyond his personal means and that it could not readily be borrowed for such a precarious undertaking. But was there not another way? Suddenly the whole problem resolved itself and the grand strategy of the revolution took shape in Bunau-Varilla's mind.

It was foolish, he saw, to waste time, money, and effort in defending the hinterlands of Panama from the federal forces that must move against the insurrectos as soon as independence was declared. The vast majority of the population of the Department of Panama lived within gunshot of the Panama Railroad. It was there that the Colombian government must strike if it hoped to quell the revolt. And had he not seen, in 1885, United States marines landed at Colón to prevent a clash between federal troops and Panama revolutionists? Just a year before, in 1902, had not Washington denied the use of the Panama Railroad to federal troops seeking to suppress an insurrection on the isthmus? All the revolting Panamanians had to do was to stay within gunshot of the Panama Railroad and they were automatically assured of United States intervention.

On reaching New York again, Bunau-Varilla immediately presented this conception to Amador. It was a less flamboyant revolution than the doctor had visualized, yet after some wavering he agreed.

"Your revolution can be financed for $100,000," said Bunau-Varilla. "This sum I shall advance from my personal fortune. Prepare to leave on the next steamer for the isthmus."

For three days Bunau-Varilla busied himself with the details of the revolution. Understanding well the temperament of the isthmians, he left no detail to chance. The declaration of Panama independence he wrote out in full; he drew up a program for the military operations of the revolution; he outlined the constitution for the new government; he designed a flag for the new republic; and he drafted a cable to be transmitted by the junta, designating him Minister Plenipotentiary and instructing him to negotiate with the United States for a canal treaty. All this Bunau-Varilla did in Room 1162 of the old Waldorf Astoria in New York City. As soon as he had finished, he thrust the documents into the hands of the bewildered Amador and bundled him off to a steamer. Then followed days of anxious waiting—the daring scheme was promising enough but already Colombia had massed troops at Cartagena.

The ensuing revolution, while it followed the basic plan conceived by Bunau-Varilla, only succeeded through further interpositions from New

York. In these the agile Bunau-Varilla acted, in the eyes of the revolutionists, as their intermediary with the Washington government. As a matter
of fact he, of course, had no such status, either actually or tacitly. But he
did take advantage with uncanny prescience of the more or less inevitable reaction of the United States to the brewing disturbances at Panama.
This reaction was based, not primarily on interest in the projected waterway, but rather on a historic policy toward the Panama Railway. To the
revolutionists, however, it appeared in quite a different light, a misappre-
hension which Bunau-Varilla did not attempt to dispel. What actually
happened was bizarre in the extreme.

The revolutionists, fearful of the Colombian troops gathered at Cartagena, cabled in code that they could not launch the insurrection unless
a United States ship was sent to their aid. Bunau-Varilla went to Washington and talked with certainty of his influential friends who, of course,
were ignorant of his connection with the revolt. Everyone sensed trouble
at Panama. From what he learned by indirection, he produced a shrewdly
accurate deduction. On the way back to New York he stopped off at
Baltimore and dispatched a message to the isthmus. In two and a half
days he informed the revolutionists an American man-of-war would be
at Colón; within four days cruisers would reach Panama City.

On the day indicated, November 2, the USS *Nashville* reached Colón
from Kingston. The ship came over the horizon late in the afternoon, all
unwittingly conveying to the anxiously waiting revolutionists a fulfillment
of Bunau-Varilla's cabled promise. The sight of the *Nashville,* still far out
at sea, was the spark that lighted the smoldering revolt. With the sup-
posed backing of the United States Navy, the Panamanians could laugh
at the whole Colombian army. Although our government acted without
the slightest collusion with the revolutionists, the result of its action was
to bring the Republic of Panama into being. Bunau-Varilla had taken a
magnificent gamble, and he won. Then emerged in brief career Bunau-
Varilla, the statesman.

The promise of the post as Minister to Washington he had thought-
fully exacted in advance. The pledge was reluctantly fulfilled, for once

the revolution had succeeded there was a very understandable objection to the detail of a foreigner, one assumed to be so closely connected with the United States, to represent the isthmus in the approaching canal negotiations. But Bunau-Varilla was not pro-United States. He was the disciple of an idea. He insistently assumed the duties of Envoy Extraordinary and Minister Plenipotentiary of the Republic of Panama and then proceeded to deliver the culminating stroke in his long struggle for the vindication of De Lesseps.

Bunau-Varilla had by this time acquired a good working knowledge of American politics. He had witnessed Hay's treaty troubles with the Senate, particularly in the instance of the first Hay-Pauncefote Treaty. He had learned that the best statesman is sometimes the best politician. He determined to write a treaty that would satisfy Hay but which would also meet every senatorial objection and to have it ratified at Panama. The result was the Hay-Bunau-Varilla treaty. This treaty gave the United States complete sovereign rights over the entire Canal Zone. It insured the neutrality of the waterway and non-discrimination in the matter of tolls. It indemnified Panama on the same basis as previously provided to Colombia in the unratified Hay-Harran treaty. It bears the imprint of broad statesmanship. It stands today a continuing monument to the genius of the man who wrote it and who saw it past the legislative reefs of Washington and Panama.

The Hay-Bunau-Varilla treaty was ratified by the Senate after extended debate by a vote of 75 to 17. On February 26, 1904, the ratifications were formally exchanged between President Roosevelt and Minister Bunau-Varilla. The same day the Frenchman resigned his diplomatic post and turned away to watch from the side lines the materialization of the idea to which he had dedicated the best years of his life. Among the many testimonials which Bunau-Varilla carried from the scene of his triumphs was a letter from the Parisian publicist, E. Regnault. It closes with the fitting epitome,

I do not congratulate you. I merely say to you, in all sincerity, you are a great man.

"The Panama Canal"

2

R. E. Bakenhus, Civil Engineer, USN

U.S. Naval Institute *Proceedings*
(Volume 1—1913): 599–676

EDITOR'S NOTE: *This wonderfully comprehensive article is too large for this anthology—at nearly 30,000 words, it would take up too much available space at the expense of other worthwhile articles. Accordingly, it has been abridged. Extracted portions are flagged for the reader's information by ellipses.*

THERE COULD BE NO BETTER INTRODUCTION to an article on the Panama Canal than the enthusiastic words of Ambassador Bryce in a recent chapter on the Isthmus of Panama, where he says, in referring to the canal:

There is something in the magnitude and the methods of this enterprise which a poet might take as his theme. Never before on our planet have so much labour, so much scientific knowledge, and so much executive skill been concentrated on a work designed to bring the nations nearer to one another and serve the interests of all mankind.

In no previous age could an enterprise so vast as this have been carried through; that is to say, it would have required a time so long and an expenditure so prodigious that no rational government would have attempted it.

It is true we have elsewhere done work of comparable magnitude—the tunnels under the Hudson and East Rivers, the great railroads and terminals, the Erie Canal, the city subways and water-supply systems, the reclamation projects and great bridges—but these are all intimately interwoven with our daily life and progress. The canal is a project crystallized from the vast multitude of enterprises and is indisputably the greatest of them all.

With a subject so vast, and one that has attained historic interest and ranks as an engineering work of such magnitude, it seems necessary to give a resume of the early history, and consider it in connection with events that may be well known in other connections. . . .

General Description of the Canal

The sea-level approach channel from the Caribbean Sea lies within Limon Bay for 42 miles. It is 500 feet wide on the bottom, with side slopes of one vertical to three horizontal, and having a depth of 4½ feet below mean sea-level. The range of the tide is about 2 feet. The alignment is straight for 5½ miles from the entrance as far as the Mindi Hills, at which point the American canal intersects the comparatively insignificant old French canal. There is a slight bend of long radius at Midi Hills, and then a straight run of 1½ miles to Gatun Locks. We have passed from the valley of the Midi River into the valley of the Chagres, and are face to face with one of the great problems of the canal construction, namely, the handling of the torrential Chagres River. After weighing several other schemes, that finally adopted consists of the formation of a lake measuring about 24 miles on the canal axis from Gatun to Bas Obispo. The length of the lake in the other direction will be over 30 miles. The lake is formed by the construction of an earth dam of unusual dimensions extending across the valley at Gatun. The dam does not seem artificial to the eye, but appears as one of the major features of the landscape. After the lake is filled, the flow of the Chagres into it will be discharged by the carefully designed concrete spillway, which cuts through the middle of the great earth dam at a point where a rocky eminence afforded a safe location. The normal water-surface of Gatun Lake will be 85 feet above mean sea-level, but provisions are made so that the water-surface can be carried at any elevation between 80 feet and 87 feet.

Ships will be passed into Gatun Lake by means of a series of three locks at Gatun, each of which in turn will raise the vessel an average of 28⅓ feet. The locks are close together and the ships will pass directly from one lock into the next. The three locks are in duplicate; that is, a vessel may go up either one flight or the other of the duplicate locks, or one flight may be used for ascending vessels and the other for descending vessels. The corresponding locks adjoin and there is only a dividing wall between them. After the ship has passed into the lower lock, and while it is being raised, the following ship, if close behind, may be tied up at the approach wall 1200 feet long, formed by an extension of the dividing wall. Each lock has a net or usable length of 1000 feet, and a net or usable width of 110 feet, but the dimensions of the ship must be somewhat less than this to provide for clearances.

The formation of the lake with the water 85 feet above the sea-level obviated all digging for 17 miles, except the top of an occasional mound. The alignment of the channel in the lake was determined by the position of hills, changed into islands by the rising water.

At the locks, the canal axis makes a slight bend to the left and the channel of 1000 feet width and 75 feet depth extends in a straight line for 3½ miles to the first bend in the lake. This bend is followed by a straight channel of the same width but reduced depth for a distance of 4½ miles, almost to Bohio, where a further turn to the left is made. The course does not run straight to Bohio from the locks, because Tiger Hill and Lion Hill are in the way. After a two-mile run from Bohio to Buena Vista, 1000 feet wide, there is a turn to the right, the course continuing straight for a distance of 272 miles to a point opposite Frijoles. Here there is a further turn to the right, with a straight course of 2½ miles, still 1000 feet wide, to a point near Tabernilla; then a turn to the left, with a reduction in width to 800 feet, and a straight reach of 3 miles to a point near San Pablo. The lake has now become a narrow arm, occupying the region where the valley of the Chagres had much steeper banks. At San Pablo there is a turn to the left with a short run 800 feet wide of one mile; then a turn to the right, another short run of 1 mile, with a further turn to the right; then a longer reach of 3 miles, with width reduced to 500 feet, passing the submerged town of Gorgona; then a right turn and a 1-mile run to a point near Gamboa. From Gatun to Gamboa there are 23 crossings of the former course of the Chagres, showing that the canal has practically followed the course of the river, but with the aid of steam shovels has selected a much straighter course than the one carved by the river along the lines of least resistance.

At Bas Obispo, which is close to Gamboa, we enter the great Culebra Cut. The minimum width of the canal up to this point has been 500 feet, but through the following 8.1 miles the bottom width is reduced to 300 feet to save excavation. The banks of the canal become higher and higher as we pass on, until at Gold Hill, the elevation of the highest land on one side is 554 feet above sea-level, and the other side, 410 feet, while the land over the center of the canal was formerly 312 feet above sea-level, or 227 feet above the bottom of the canal. The minimum depth of the canal on the entire upper level is 45 feet at normal lake-level, or 40 feet at low lake-level, but throughout Gatun Lake the depth is in excess of these. The Culebra Cut and the 85-foot elevation of the water both end at the Pedro Miguel Lock. In passing through the cut, from Bas Obispo to Pedro Miguel, there are eight straight reaches connected by easy curves, three to the right and four to the left. It is most remarkable that so large a portion of this run is on straight lines, and that the total degree of curvature has been kept so low.

At Pedro Miguel there is one lock in duplicate which lowers the vessel to the 55-foot elevation of Miraflores Lake. The Pedro Miguel Lock has approach walls formed by 1200-foot extensions in both directions of the dividing-wall between the locks. Miraflores Lake is comparatively small, and a run of 12 miles, in a 500-foot channel 45 feet deep, takes the ship to Miraflores. At this point there are two locks in duplicate, with approach walls at the upper and lower levels, the same as at Pedro Miguel and Gatun. The two locks at Miraflores lower the vessel to tidewater, a drop of 45 feet at high tide, or 65 feet at low tide. The 20-foot tides on the Pacific coast have made the problem more difficult than on the Atlantic coast, where the tide is only 2 feet. One-half mile beyond Miraflares Locks the canal makes a turn to the right and extends for a distance of 2½ miles to Balboa, where it makes a turn to the left and extends for 4½ miles to deep water in the Bay of Panama. The Pacific sea-level section is all of 500 feet width, and the depth of the water is 55 feet at high tide and 35 feet at low tide, and is usually stated to be 45 feet deep, referring to mean tide.

The total length of the canal, measured along its axis, is 50.4 miles. The portion within the shore lines is only 41.5 miles, and the remainder consists of dredged channels in Limon Bay and Panama Bay. Of the total length, 14½ miles are at sea-level, over 23½ miles in Gatun Lake, nearly 3 miles in the locks or alongside approach walls, 1½ miles in Miraflores Lake and 8 miles in the Culebra Cut. In the total length there are 22 bends, with a total curvature of 600 degrees and 51 minutes. The average length of the straight reach is a little over 2 miles. At each bend the canal is widened by cutting away on the inside of the bend, the shape and amount of cutting having been determined after observations of vessels actually rounding turns.

The time required for a vessel to pass through is estimated to be from 10 to 12 hours, of which 3 hours is required for passing the locks. Through the Culebra Cut the vessel must reduce speed, but for most of the remaining distance may approach full speed.

Gatun Lake

Less attention, it is believed, has been paid to Gatun Lake by those describing the canal than the subject really deserves. It forms the preponderant element in the American project. The great dam at Gatun, the spillway, and the locks are only incidental to the lake, and by virtue of it the amount of excavation and the attendant difficulties in the Culebra Cut are greatly reduced.

The lake provides 23½ miles of canal channel, or nearly half the total length, and gives a width of 1000 feet for 16 miles, 800 feet for 4 miles, and 500 feet for the remaining 4 miles; the average width is nearly 900 feet, while the rest of the canal averages less than 450 feet. Not only in width, but also in depth the lake channel offers an advantage, for while the rest of the channel is limited to an ample depth of 45 feet, the lake offers a maximum depth of about 75 feet, and is nowhere less than 45 feet along the navigable channel. These generous dimensions will facilitate navigation and will allow vessels to approach their ocean speed.

Besides being such a valuable asset to navigation, Gatun Lake solves one of the most difficult and most vital of all the problems involved in the canal construction. We are familiar with the characteristics of the Chagres River. This wild and variable stream is immediately tamed and calmed on entering Gatun Lake. Its waters, which form and replenish the lake, may be likened to a beast of burden quietly carrying the ships to and fro, supplying the lifting force that passes them through the locks, and the power to drive the generators which light the canal, operate the machinery, and may later operate the railroad.

While great ideas and great accomplishments may be briefly abstracted in picturesque terms, the knowledge so given is superficial if unaccompanied by a more intimate consideration of the principles involved, and of the studies and investigations which attended them. Nothing may be left to surmise or conjecture, no assumptions may be made, unsupported by masses of the best evidence available. Where the problems are new and no direct evidence can be obtained, the best engineering judgment, based on experience, must be brought into play.

An investigation had first to be made as to the sufficiency of the water-supply. The lake, once it is formed, will suffer losses from at least five different sources: 1st, evaporation; 2d, seepage, or groundflow; 3d, leakage through the lock gates and spillway gates; 4th, water required to pass ships through the locks; and 5th, water to develop power, if a sufficient amount remains available.

Evaporation depends on the wind and the hygrometric state of the air, and also on the area of the lake. At the normal elevation of 85 feet above sea-level, the area of the lake is 163 square miles. For certain reasons that will be discussed later the elevation of the lake may, when actually placed in service, vary from 80 to 90 feet above sea-level, and the area of the lake will vary correspondingly from 153 to 173 square miles. Evaporation continues from day to day, and unfortunately is the greatest when rainfall is the least. The length of the dry season is therefore of importance. To provide for the driest future year, the weather records as far back as available are studied, and the driest year taken as a standard, with an allowance for even more unfavorable conditions. Fortunately, the French under the New Company made continuous and careful observations of all meteorological and hydrological features of value. The Americans have continued these observations with great care and completeness. Evaporation pans have also been exposed to secure direct evidence which would bear some relation to the rate of evaporation from the lake. From the best evidence available, the probable rate of evaporation is found to be about one-fourth of an inch per 24 hours. This has been computed to equal a loss of 930 cubic feet per second.

The loss by seepage is dependent on the character of the soil forming the bottom of the lake, and of the head or pressure of water at any particular point. To clearly understand its character we may note that an ordinary river in reality includes more than the flowing water which is visible between its banks, in that the ground along the river contains water which to the eye seems quiescent, but which actually has a flow, extremely slow, but always moving toward the river and down the valley with the river. Its rate of flow depends on the character of the material, the frictional resistance, and the distance to be traveled; it is comparatively rapid in sand or gravel, and is reduced to a minimum in clays and rocks. The seepage from Gatun Lake will be of an allied nature, and it remains to estimate the amount. The engineers made careful studies of the bottom of the lake by borings, test pits, and geological surveys. Specially careful examinations were made at those points where the ridges between the lake and the adjoining valleys are narrow and low. It was perfectly possible that gravel strata or porous coral deposits might exist which, communicating with the sea, might discharge the waters of the lake as through a sieve. The engineers satisfied themselves that no such condition existed, and their judgment was confirmed by a Board of Consulting Engineers appointed in 1908 by President Roosevelt. The probable seepage was estimated to be 85 cubic feet per second, or less than one-tenth the rate of evaporation during the dry season.

The loss of water through leaks and imperfect seatings in the many valves and miter-gates of the locks, and the 14 gates of the spillway, depends on the accuracy with which the devices are made, and the care used in the maintenance. The commission followed correct principles in using the utmost care in designing and constructing them, and yet assuming a rather heavy loss of water from incomplete closure or accident. The amount lost is estimated to be 275 cubic feet per second, the equivalent of 20 city fire streams.

The amount of water found necessary for developing electric current for lighting the canal, and operating all the machinery, is estimated at 275 cubic feet per second, based on the required amount of current and the efficiency of the apparatus.

The amount of water required for lockages is dependent on the design of the locks, the amount of traffic, and the size of the vessels, for the locks are so divided that small vessels may use short sections, or several small vessels pass through the whole lock together. Assuming the traffic equal to the maximum capacity of the locks, and utilizing records of experience with the Sault Ste. Marie Canal, the Board of Consulting Engineers estimated the traffic at 80,000,000 register tons per year, as against 30,000,000 tons for the "Soo" Canal, and an actual maximum of

15,500,000 tons for the Suez. The amount of water required for lockage was found by the designing engineers to be 2618 cubic feet per second, which means about one lockage in each direction per hour, but the assumed maximum traffic will not be reached for many years.

Adding the total losses from all causes gives a total of 4183 cubic feet per second, applicable during the dry months, when evaporation is the greatest. The question now arises: Where is this rather enormous quantity of water coming from? The input into Gatun Lake comes from rainfall directly on the lake, which is absent in the dry season, however, and from the flow of Chagres River and of minor streams. The data desired for this purpose pertains to the driest period that may be reasonably expected, and the best way to predict it is from records of the flow of the Chagres in past years. The records of the New French Panama Canal Company furnish much reliable information, while that obtained from the old company is fragmentary and incomplete.

The driest consecutive four months in the available records of 19 years show a flow on an average of 1190 cubic feet per second into the lake. Unfortunately, a 19-year period is hardly sufficient to determine the future probable minimum, and the average of 1190 cubic feet which occurred in 1908, the year the computations were made, was followed in 1912 by an average flow for four months of less than 900 cubic feet per second, or about 25 per cent less. This will not affect the problem adversely, because of the liberal allowances made in determining losses and the possibility of using the Miraflores oil-fired steam plant in place of water-power.

It is apparent that the 1190 cubic feet per second supplied to Gatun Lake will not provide the 4183 cubic feet per second to be consumed. The balance, or 2993 cubic feet per second, will be obtained by filling Gatun Lake to a level of 87 feet above the sea (the gates and copings are 92 feet) before the end of the rainy season, and then during the succeeding dry season, drawing the lake down gradually to a level of 80 feet above sea-level, if need be. The storage capacity of the lake between these two levels, at an average area of about 159 square miles, will supply this amount of water with a slight margin. The problem is identical in many respects with that involved in the great impounding reservoirs of modern city waterworks, such as those of Boston and New York, where storage tides over the dry season.

It may be noted that this drawing off of the upper 5 feet of the lake explains one reason why the depth of channel through the Culebra Cut was made 45 feet at normal lake level. The water level in the cut is the same as in the lake, and when the lake falls to 80 feet, the channel in the cut will have 40 feet depth of water.

At this point it becomes clear that one of the greatest responsibilities of the canal operating force will be the conservation of the water. The operator must be thoroughly versed in problems of rainfall and hydrology, and should begin the dry season with a full lake, and he must be careful not to be caught by an unexpectedly early or unusually dry season; he must each year be prepared for the worst. No apprehension need be felt that the water-supply will give out, however, if reasonable care is taken. Should more water be required to meet new conditions of the distant future, it may be obtained by building a reservoir on the upper Chagres, with a dam at Alhajuela, where some of the floodwaters of the Chagres may be stored until needed in the dry season. It was here that the French proposed building a reservoir for supplying the highest level of their canal through a tunnel.

We have seen that Gatun Lake can be kept full, but have yet to determine that it can be filled initially. An examination of the records of flow of the Chagres for all available years leaves no doubt that the water in the rainy season in excess of all losses is more than sufficient to fill the lake in two successive years. The driest rainy season of record, 1911–1912, afforded an average flow of 6556 cubic feet per second, which would have filled Gatun Lake in about 400 days, or two rainy seasons, making deductions for reduced losses on account of there being no lockages, no hydraulic power plant in operation, and less evaporation, leaks and seepage, due to reduced lake area and head of water.

The Gatun Dam

The Gatun Dam, which made Gatun Lake possible, is the key to the American Panama Canal scheme. The lock-level canal might have been built with a dam at a different location, such as that proposed by the French at Bohio, but the area of the lake would have been very much less, with a consequent loss of opportunity to navigate in wide, unrestricted channels, and a great loss in storage capacity. The dam at Bohio could have been built of masonry on a rock foundation, for which the French made considerable excavation. A masonry dam on rock foundation was not possible at Gatun, because the rock is too far below the surface. It was only after advice had been obtained of some of the ablest engineering talent in the world, familiar with similar problems elsewhere that an earth dam at Gatun was decided on. This decision was probably the most momentous one in connection with the canal construction. Elaborate investigations were made of the character of the underlying material through test pits and innumerable borings. It was found that the top layer consisted of fine sand intermixed with a large proportion of clay, which extended to a maximum depth at one point of practically 80 feet. Below this, for a distance of 50 feet or more, is a thick deposit of impervious blue clay, containing a little sand with a quantity of shells interspersed. Below the clay, and directly overlying the bed rock, is a miscellaneous layer of variable thickness up to 20 feet, consisting of boulders and gravel consolidated with finely divided clays and silts.

Several important factors enter into the design of this dam and the determination of its dimensions. The dam itself must be impervious to water, or on finer analysis it would be more accurate to say the seepage must be a minimum. If a well, extending below the ordinary level of the ground water, and without tapping subterranean water channels, is pumped, the ground water in the surrounding territory will flow towards the well and its level will gradually fall and assume a curve joining the surface of the water in the well with the normal ground-water level some distance away. The slope of this curve depends upon the character of the material and the amount of friction which it exerts against the flow. Deeper pumping will lower the curve and extend it farther back. To maintain a fixed level of water in the well will require a fixed rate of pumping, equal to the seepage through the ground, so long as no rain falls on the area affected by the well. The conditions at the Gatun Dam are similar, with the ground-water level in the valley below the dam corresponding to the water in the well and the water in the lake corresponding to the normal ground-water level, and the slope curve passing through the dam.

To prevent loss of water, the materials of which the dam is built must be selected from the available local deposits and placed in such a way as to retard to the greatest possible extent the flow of water. In very fine silts the rate of flow is so minute that they are generally classed as impervious. Capillary attraction is a force which must be considered. It is this which keeps the surface of ordinary ground moist. The evaporation from the surface removes the moisture, but it is promptly replaced by capillary attraction from the ground-water reservoir below. With no rain the ground water is thus gradually lowered until the capillary forces are no longer sufficient to raise the water to the surface, which then becomes dry. This force must also be considered, although to a minor extent, in the design of the dam.

Unfortunately, the ordinary materials which are classed as impervious have a faculty for absorbing water, which softens them and reduces their capacity for self-support. With the height of water furnished by Gatun Lake there is ample opportunity for the contents of the dam to become saturated, and materials subject to disintegration, or with a tendency to absorb, would not maintain the side slopes. Clay or fine silt is particularly treacherous in its nature; yet it is upon these materials that the imperviousness of Gatun Dam must depend. The solution of this problem is to build the center of the dam of impervious material and the outer portion on both sides of a material capable of maintaining the predetermined slopes wet or dry, but necessarily allowing water to pass. On the lake side it must be faced with a lining to resist wave action.

Yet this is not all. The weight of the dam might produce so great a pressure on the original surface of the earth that it would sink and cause the earth to rise just beyond the toe of the dam. This actually happened only a short distance away with embankments for the Panama Railroad. The remedy was to counterweight the rising area of soft material at the toe of the embankment with fill material and thus prevent any further rise. With a structure like the Gatun Dam, settlement of this character would have dislodged the parts of the dam already built, would have created possible fissures and avenues for future flow, and would have aroused the greatest doubt in the minds of the public as to its strength and safety; therefore, the question must be investigated and settled in advance. The rising of the material is prevented by first removing any soft material, and further by making the dam very wide, with a thin extended toe, thus making the counterweight a part of the dam itself. Even with the greatest precautions a slip in the rock fill due to giving way of soft material near the old French canal occurred and caused great popular alarm, and led the President to order a board of eminent engineers to Panama. Their report was most reassuring and confirmed in the main the judgment of the commission.

Not only the dam itself, but also the material upon which it is built, must prevent the water from flowing underneath it. To increase imperviousness, the commission drove a line of sheet piling twenty feet into the earth; but on the advice of the special board of engineers this was omitted and, instead, a trench was dug along the middle, which was filled by the core of the dam.

The generous dimensions of the dam, however, principally contribute the imperviousness and stability. As finally built the crest is 100 feet wide and 20 feet above normal water-level; the thickness of the dam at the water-surface is 400 feet, and it increases to a thickness of nearly one-half mile at its deepest part.

The dam, after clearing the 573 acres of site, was constructed by first building long mounds along the outer lines of the dam with the proper exterior slope. The material was spoil from the Culebra Cut, the locks and the spillway, and was dumped from trestles. When the mounds were carried to sufficient height, the interior space was filled with silty material from nearby deposits by the hydraulic dredging process. Where the course of the Chagres crosses the dam two lines of sheet piling were driven, and the material between them, which was not of a suitable character, was excavated and replaced.

The design of the Gatun Dam was not decided on until elaborate tests had been made of the actual seepage through the material to be used in the construction. These seepage tests were made by drilling holes into the deposits that were later to form the core of the dam, and pumping a measured amount of water into them and noting the loss and rate of flow under fixed pressures. The natural flow of the ground water through the soil was also studied. Several model dams were built and experiments made to determine the slope of the water through the material of the dam, caused by the miniature lake on one side. Test pits were dug in the deposits, and the flow into the test pits was pumped out and measured, while at the same time observations on the level of the ground water were taken in the neighborhood.

The dimensions of the cross-section of the dam were twice changed. The height of 135 feet above sea-level, as originally proposed, was at first reduced to 115 feet, and finally to the adopted height of 105 feet. The surface slopes and width at the bottom were also changed.

Gatun Spillway

During the rainy season the influx of water into Gatun Lake will be much greater than the amount consumed, and the spillway through the Gatun Dam provides the outlet. It might have been placed anywhere on the rim of the lake and a channel to the sea constructed, but a favorable site on rock foundation was found on the line of the dam, which allowed the use of the bed of the Chagres for carrying the water to the sea.

The spillway consists of a concrete dam with means for overflow, and a concrete channel to lead the water away. It is a most important adjunct to Gatun Lake, for it not only will safely relieve the lake of dangerous flood-waters, but also will control the level of the water-surface, thus accomplishing the storage of a part of the flood-waters for use in the dry season. Its discharge capacity must be made equal to that of the greatest possible flood. To determine the amount of water, we must again seek information in the records of the New French Company and the succeeding records by the Americans. It is to be deplored that the old company obtained no record of the Chagres flood of 1879, known to be larger than any covered by subsequent records. The engineers' report states that, "The maximum momentary discharge of the Chagres River at Gatun is calculated from the measured Bohio discharge to be 182,000 cubic feet per second." This is over 200 times the minimum dry-weather flow.

An overflow type of spillway to carry off this amount of water would be over 2,000 feet long, and even so its discharge capacity at the highest floods would not be sufficient, and the lake might rise five feet. For these reasons the commission adopted a spillway with a crest that is semicircular in plan and has fourteen openings cut through the upper part, closed by gates. The elevation of the bottom of the openings is at 69 feet above sea-level, or 16 feet below the normal level of the lake. Each opening is about 45 feet wide. They are so wide, in fact, that the top of the spillway is really composed of a series of piers, with the openings containing the valves between them. When the gate is shut, its top is at elevation 88 above sea-level, making the gate 19 feet in its vertical dimensions. The gate may be raised 22½ feet, or clear of a 90-foot depth of water in the lake. This device for discharging water from the lake is far superior to the plain crest without gates, because the amount of water passing through may be very nicely controlled; furthermore, any increase in the depth of the water in the lake from sudden floods would tend to increase the capacity of each opening of the spillway, because the amount of water discharged through a weir is dependent upon the head or elevation of water which is acting on the weir.

When the lake is at elevation 87 a single gate will discharge 11,000 cubic feet per second, or 154,000 cubic feet per second for the lot. The maximum known flow of the Chagres is less than this amount; in fact, is only 137,500 cubic feet for any prolonged period, such as 33 hours. The momentary discharge may be much greater than this and has been determined as high as 186,000 cubic feet per second, but, in designing a spillway, the momentary maximum is not what is wanted. Should any flood occur which will exceed the capacity of 154,000 cubic feet per second, then, of course, the lake will begin to rise; but as it rises, the capacity of the spillway is increased until, with the lake at the improbable elevation of 92 feet, above which the water would flow over the miter-gates and into the locks, the rate of discharge of the crest will be 222,000 cubic feet per second. In addition to this, water can be passed through the lock culverts both at Gatun and Pedro Miguel. The length of the period over which records of flow of the Chagres are available is insufficient to predict with any degree of certainty the probable maximum flood at some future time, and the commission has again shown its wisdom in designing for a capacity which is quite far in advance of that required by recorded floods.

The gates themselves are constructed of heavy and massive steel work. They are of the so-called Stoney gate-valve type. The sliding frictional resistance of ordinary valves of this size would be very great. The Stoney pattern of valves overcomes this by using roller trains upon which the valve travels. Passing lengthwise along the dam and underneath the gates is a tunnel in which all the machinery for operating the gate valves is placed. A chain is fastened to each side of the gate and passes over a sprocket-wheel on the adjoining pier, and then down through a vertical well to the machinery tunnel. A large screw is fastened to the end of the chain and passes through a worm. A heavy counterweight hangs on the lower end of this screw rod, leaving only frictional resistance to be overcome. The motor for operating the worms is located midway between the screw rods, thus applying equal lifting force to each end of the gate.

After passing over the crest the water slides over the face of the spillway, which is so designed as to fit the normal curve of the water. At the bottom the concrete work is curved so as to give the stream a horizontal direction. About 21 baffle piers are built within this area to retard the rapid flow. At the same time, the channel becomes contracted from a width of 414 feet, which is the length of the inside of the crest, to a width of 285 feet. The water is carried in a long sluice-way, lined with heavy concrete walls and paved with a concrete floor, and is discharged at a safe distance from the dam into the bed of the Chagres River, whence it continues to the sea. During the dry season of four months very little water will pass through the spillway, but in the rainy season varying amounts will pass. The average flow will be about 10,000 cubic feet per second, increased momentarily to almost 15 times that amount during periods of high flood. Over the tops of the piers which separate the gate openings a bridge and roadway have been built, so that traffic may be carried the full length of the Gatun Dam.

So important to the success of the canal is this spillway that the commission's engineers constructed a model of the same for experimental purposes, $\frac{1}{32}$ of the size of the original. It was tested under various conditions and the facts thus gained were of value in making the final designs. . . .

Miraflores Lake

Miraflores Lake is a very much smaller body of water than Gatun Lake, and lies between the locks at Pedro Miguel and those at Miraflores. It is a little over 1½ miles long and about 1½ miles wide at its widest part. It was at first intended to have the lower locks built close to Balboa instead of at Miraflores. If this had been done, the lake would have had an area of 7 square miles instead of as built, only one square mile, and would have afforded a very fine navigable channel of 5 miles, instead of only 1½ miles, as at the present time. This was the scheme proposed by the Board of Consulting Engineers in their report of 1906. The change from the board's plan to the one finally adopted involved an increased cost of about $10,000,000.00, and was apparently disadvantageous, so far as the physical characteristics of the canal are concerned. The reasons for the change were that close to Balboa the locks would be subject to hostile gun-fire from the Bay of Panama, and that the preliminary work on the dam at Balboa connecting with Sosa Hill showed that the most suitable foundation did not exist.

The water-level of Miraflores Lake will be carried at elevation 55 feet above mean tide. Miraflores Lake occupies a portion of the valley of the Rio Grande River, and at its lower end the Miraflores locks have been constructed in the line of this valley. Dams extend from the lock walls to neighboring hills, which are close by, so as to enclose the lake. The dam on the west side of the locks makes an apparently unnecessary sweep to the south, but the object is to capture the flow of the Cocoli River for use in the lake and to prevent the water from giving trouble in the valley below the locks. The flow from the Rio Grande and Pedro Miguel rivers, and one or two other smaller streams, also enters the lake. The water from Gatun Lake which is used in the single lock at Pedro Miguel will flow into Miraflores Lake. The water consumption from Miraflores Lake is that due to evaporation and lockages through the two sets of locks at Miraflores, and the amount used will be in excess of the supply from the rivers during the dry season. The difference will be made up from water allowed to flow into Miraflores Lake from Gatun Lake. During the rainy season there may be an excess of water, and this will be discharged through a spillway having gates exactly like those for the Gatun Dam spillway. The capacity of the gates was not, however, designed from the estimated flow thus obtained, but was based on the flow which would enter Miraflores Lake in case all the gates in one of the Pedro Miguel locks should be wrecked, and the full head of water from Gatun Lake should flow uninterruptedly through one of the Pedro Miguel locks. The discharge from the spillway is into the old channel of the Rio Grande River, over which the spillway is built. After following the old channel for about one mile, the water will be carried through the Rio Grande diversion for about 1¾ miles, when it will again enter a part of the old river channel and find its way to the sea close to the mouth of the canal.

The Canal Locks

The passage of a vessel through locks wherein it remains continually water-borne is comparatively simple, as compared with the usual process of placing vessels in dry dock, involving the removal of water from the dock and support of the ship on blocking. The percentage of accidents in both cases is found to be exceedingly small. About 90 per cent of the accidents in locking vessels is due to failure of signals from the bridge to the engine room, and these will be eliminated at Panama through the adoption of a part of the process in common use in docking; namely, the vessel will not move into the lock under its own steam but will come to a full stop at the approach wall, and the movement of the ship will then be controlled by the lock operatives. Two lines to the bow and two to the stern will be used, the strains being obtained from four electric locomotives with winches on board, running on rack railroads on the edge of the lock walls, two on each side of the lock. For large ships more lines and more locomotives may be found necessary. The process is not dissimilar to towing canal boats, but with amplifications. With experience there will no doubt be developed the proper order of seamanship to handle vessels expeditiously under these novel conditions.

The canal has in all twelve lock chambers, two flights of three each at Gatun, two flights of one each at Pedro Miguel, and two flights of two each at Miraflores. The twelve locks are alike in their principal features, but variations occur from differences in arrangements of gates and protective devices. The lock chamber must have at least one gate at each end, to separate it from the adjoining chamber or from the adjoining body of water. The minimum number of gates that would fulfill this condition for the arrangement of locks adopted is 18. The actual number used is, for various reasons to be explained later, increased to 46.

Each lock has a chamber 100 feet wide and 1000 feet long, but as about 95 per cent of all ocean-going vessels are under 600 feet long, the locks are divided by a second set of gates into two Parts, one 400 feet long and the other 600 feet long. There is no saving of time in filling a small chamber rather than the full 1000-foot lock, since all filling is done at the rate of 2 feet per minute; but advantage in the use of divided locks arises from the great saving in water, which is an element of importance, as we have seen in considering Gatun Lake. This feature adds ten pairs of lock gates to the installation. One duplicate lock, namely the lower one at Miraflores, is not provided with the dividing gates. This is because the designing engineers found that the cost of the gates and additional length of concrete structure in this particular lock, due to tidal conditions, outweighed the saving in water.

Should a vessel approaching the first lock of any flight not come to a stop through some misunderstanding, a collision with the lock gate will be prevented by a chain of 3-inch iron stretched from one side of the lock to the other. The impact will be taken up by hydraulic cylinders in the lock walls to which the ends of the chain will be attached. The resistance is sufficient to stop a 10,000-ton vessel moving at 4 knots per hour in a length of 73 feet. When not in use the chain will rest in a groove in the floor and side walls. If the chain should give way, or not be in position, the impact would be received by a pair of guard or safety gates, which it is expected would check the vessel and prevent it from injuring the next set of gates. Should the inconceivable accident happen of a vessel passing both the guard chain and safety gate and wrecking the next one while all the other gates in the lock were open, due to a vessel having just passed through, then Gatun Lake would begin to flow out to the full capacity of the channel now formed by the lock, and similarly for Lake Miraflores. Four guard gates are required to protect the entrances to the four lock chambers adjoining Gatun Lake at Gatun and Pedro Miguel, and four more to protect the exits from the same locks, as an accident at the exits would have the same consequences as at the entrances. Similarly, two gates each are required at the entrances and exits of the upper Miraflores lock chambers, or a total of twelve guard gates.

A guard gate is also constructed at the lower entrance of each flight of locks, and the leaves of this gate point away from the lock. Each of these gates is a guard for vessels approaching from below and also may be used in unwatering the lock.

Even the well-nigh impossible combination of circumstances described above would not wreck the canal. The mitering lock gates could of course not be closed against the flowing stream, and to stop the flow the emergency dam would be brought into play. The emergency dam is in the form of a bridge resting on a turntable on the side wall of the lock. It may be turned so as to span the lock and then be firmly bedded on each side. A series of steel girders with the upper ends fastened to the bridge would be lowered by cables into position, having the lower ends on a concrete sill provided for the purpose. Then steel plates would be forced down one by one, supported by the girders, and the opening would thus be gradually closed by a steel wall and the flow practically stopped. A floating caisson such as is used with dry docks would then be placed at the lake end of the lock on a seat provided for the purpose. The caisson carries a pumping plant for unwatering the lock, and repairs may thus be made. In the meantime traffic would use the other series of locks in both directions.

The locks are some of the most massive concrete work in the world. The dividing wall between the flights of three locks at Gatun, with the approach walls which are in extension of the dividing wall, forms a mass of concrete 60 feet thick, about 81 feet high, and over 1⅛ miles long. The approach walls are of cellular construction. The dividing wall is built with the faces vertical and is solid for over half the height. Above the solid portion the center of the wall is filled with earth, except three superimposed tunnels. The lowest tunnel is used for drainage of the upper ones, the center tunnel for electric light and power cables, and the upper one as a passageway for employees to reach the various chambers containing machinery for operating the miter-gates and the many valves. The exterior walls of the locks are of equal height with the central wall, and are from 45 feet to 50 feet thick at the floor-level; they diminish by steps on the back to a thickness of 8 feet at the top. The thickness of the floor is variable but is approximately 13 feet.

The emptying and filling of the locks is done through circular openings in the floor, each 3 feet 10⅞ inches in diameter and having an area of 12 square feet. There are five of them in each line across the lock, and the lines are spaced 32 feet to 36 feet apart. In one 1000-foot lock there are in all 105 openings with a total area of 1260 square feet. Each row of five openings communicates with a cross-tunnel under the floor. Eleven of these cross-tunnels in each lock lead to the outside wall and there open into a culvert 18 feet in diameter, without the interposition of valves. The remaining ten tunnels, alternating with the others, lead to the center wall where a cylindrical valve allows each tunnel to communicate with the culvert in the center wall, which is also 18 feet in diameter. The center-wall culvert receives the tunnels from both locks. It extends the full length of the three locks at Gatun, and at the upper end it opens into Gatun Lake, while the lower end discharges into the sea-level canal. There are control valves at each end and also in the line of the culvert at intermediate points corresponding to the locks. It is evident that, with a proper adjustment of the culvert valves, the water in any two lock chambers may be equalized by opening the cylindrical valves that allow the floor tunnels to communicate with the center culvert. This allows a very considerable saving of water in operation. With all culvert valves open, the center culvert may be used to discharge water from Gatun Lake into the sea. The side-wall culverts also extend the full length of the locks, and have control valves at the ends and at points corresponding to the ends of the locks, and at the subdivision points. They may be used in equalizing the water in any two locks that adjoin endwise, or in passing water into and out of the end locks. . . .

Locks as the Limiting Feature

The locks fix the maximum-size ship that may use the canal. They will pass the largest now built or building, but will not, for instance, pass the floating dry dock Dewey, which passed through the Suez Canal on the way to the Philippine Islands. The size of the locks was determined from the provisions of the Act of Congress approved June 28, 1902, which states: "Such canal shall be of sufficient capacity and depth as shall afford convenient passage for vessels of the largest tonnage and greatest draft now in use, and such as may be reasonably anticipated. . . ."

In considering the limiting dimensions of the locks, and thus of the canal, it must be borne in mind that there has been a steady increase in the size of ships, upon which great emphasis has been laid. If curves are plotted to show the growth in length, width, depth and tonnage, especially if the maximum ship of each period is taken, and if these curves are extended to show future developments, the predictions are alarming. However, when the curves are produced beyond a certain point other factors—not hitherto considered, and having no influence on the curves as plotted, are likely to enter. Shipbuilding has undergone an almost untrammeled development; building facilities, capital and cost have seemingly not retarded growth. Harbors have been deepened, channels have been widened, wharves, docks, locks and wet basins have been increased in size, to make way for the leviathans. The impetus toward larger vessels has undoubtedly been from economic reasons. Ship owners have found that with the larger and better equipped ships, having in view passenger traffic and advertising effects as well as freight, their ratio of income has increased and there has been nothing to curb their efforts. Communities and governments have, in their striving for all-important commercial growths, paid the bills for harbor development. As economic conditions have brought about the steep rise in the shipgrowth curve, so economic conditions, but in another field, will tend to flatten the curve. There must be a limit beyond which harbor development cannot economically go, and beyond which the sum of the cost of shipping and building and the cost of construction and maintenance of port works will increase rather than decrease. It will be difficult to determine when this point is reached, especially because the same interests do not provide capital for both enterprises. There are already occasional indications that this factor is entering. The difficulty in providing for the largest ships in New York harbor, while from one standpoint a physical one, is in the last analysis economic.

There is now no commercial necessity why the Panama Canal should accommodate the largest ships; the largest ships may be regarded as ocean ferries with fixed ports. The total estimated traffic capacity of 80,000,000 tons can be handled in ships under 600 feet long, which comprise 95 per cent of the world's tonnage, but within the next generation the canal may become one of the elements which exercise a retardant influence on the maximum size of ships, depending on developments in the commerce of the world.

More important is the effect of the canal on the size of naval vessels. Battleships of the United States have increased in beam from 76 feet in 1900 (date of authorization) to 80 feet in 1905, 88 feet in 1908, and about 98 feet in 1912; and if this ratio of increase is maintained, the limiting beam would be reached in ships authorized in about 1915.

It is worthy of note that the locks of the enlarged Kaiser Wilhelm Canal from the Baltic to the North Sea are 1082 feet long and 147 feet wide, but the lift is very much less than at Panama. . . .

Control of Water during Construction of the Canal

One of the serious problems that arose in connection with the actual construction of various parts of the canal has not been touched on in describing items such as the locks, dams, and Culebra Cut, because it can be better treated as an individual subject. We realize that the canal is built in the valleys of the Chagres and Rio Grande Rivers, and that the route selected is the very lowest one that could be found. Knowing the character of tropical rainstorms and river floods, it needs but a moment's thought to make clear the seriousness of the problem of keeping the storm waters and the floods away from the construction work. Improperly or insufficiently controlled, these waters would have the power to destroy a great deal of what had been laboriously done.

The Culebra Cut forming the low point for many square miles of territory, and coinciding for a considerable distance with the Obispo River valley, would naturally collect vast quantities of water were steps not taken to prevent it. The course of the Obispo River was artificially changed, beginning at the point where it approached the cut. The total length of the new river channel as originally built was 5¼ miles, from a point on the east side of the Culebra Cut, near the foot of Gold Hill, to a point clear of the cut, and finally discharging into the Chagres River. On account of slides encountered during construction work, the Obispo diversion gave way, and the flow of the river entered the cut for 3 days, causing inconvenience and damage. A new diversion channel was constructed with great speed. That the Obispo diversion was no small problem may be noted from the fact that in six years a total of 1,200,000 cubic yards of excavation was necessary, of which nearly 40 per cent was in rock, and the total cost was over $1,000,000.00. The diversion was able to carry 6000 cubic feet of water per second. The Camacho diversion on the opposite side of the cut was similarly built.

These two diversions take waters which flow toward the Atlantic. The Rio Grande River formerly flowed through part of the area to be excavated on the Pacific side of the Continental Divide. It was similarly diverted, and a dyke was constructed across the south end of the canal to prevent access of the river water. Keeping water out of the cut also kept out the silt which would inevitably have come down with the freshets.

The elevation of the bottom of the cut was 40 feet, which was lower than the Chagres River, and a dam was built across the cut with its crest at elevation 73 to prevent the river from flowing into it.

The natural streams being thus prevented from entering the work, it only remained to get rid of the water which originated along 8¼ miles of cut. This was done by means of centrifugal pumps at low points in the cut, which discharged the water over the dams. Excavation at a new level was always preceded by the cutting of a pioneer trench down the middle of the canal, in which all the water was collected and carried to the pumping stations. The summit during construction was at Culebra. Drainage to the south was carried to Pedro Miguel until August, 1911, when the flow was taken through the center-wall culvert of the Pedro Miguel Lock. The drainage to the north was disposed of by pumping.

The Chagres had no opportunity to interfere with the Culebra Cut, but had ample opportunity by virtue of its location, to threaten the work on the Gatun Dam. This problem was handled with ingenuity by the engineers. The portions of the dam not accessible to the river were constructed first. The spillway was built with its foundations on rock and with the river kept out by cofferdams and otherwise. In the meantime the Chagres River flowed through the west diversion built by the French. When the spillway, in 1911, had been constructed to elevation 10 feet above sea-level, and the earth dam well above this elevation, the channels of the Chagres were closed by carrying the dam across, and the water then flowed over the concrete work of the spillway during the rainy season. This depth kept the Panama Railroad, still on the old line in the Chagres valley, free of water. During the following season the railroad was transferred to the relocated or high line above the final level of Gatun Lake. The earth dam was continually kept at an elevation well above that of the concrete work of the spillway, and the next step during the dry season consisted of constructing 4 very large culverts in a part of the spillway temporarily protected from the flow of the water and controlled by gates. There were provisions for placing stop planks for closing the openings at some future time. When these culverts were completed, the dry-weather flow of the river was carried through them, and the remaining concrete work of the spillway progressed so long as the dry season lasted, and so long as the culverts were able to carry the flow. During the rainy season the flow was again over the concrete work of the spillway at elevation 50. Proceeding thus, the spillway was completed, and the final step, when the spillway is entirely done, consists in placing the stop planks before the entrance to the 4 culverts and filling them with concrete.

The Gatun Locks extend to a depth of about 55 feet below mean sea-level, and the water was kept off the site by means of a temporary dam to the north of the locks. This was built so that the excavation for the flare-walls might be done by dredges, as the material was too soft to hold steam-shovels. Inasmuch as the dredges could not dig the full depth of

70 feet, a small lake was formed over the area of the flare-walls, and its elevation was lowered until the dredge could reach the bottom. This lake was kept from flowing into the partially completed locks by means of a temporary concrete dam, built between the center and side walls near the lower end of the Gatun Locks. . . .

The Elements of Success

A consideration of the elements to which the undertaking owes its accomplishment is most important and interesting, in order to correctly comprehend how success was achieved. It must first be admitted that fortune favored us. We did not apply our determination to build the canal to actual construction work until after the world had fully developed the mosquito theory, and Cuba had given us an opportunity to apply it to practical sanitation.

Two generations of railroad building; river and harbor improvement, water-works, and other large construction, together with the coincident growth of the great technical schools, had developed a body of engineers and constructors with the technique and capacity for conceiving and executing large works, and a strongly formed spirit of loyalty and devotion that allowed them to be welded into the nucleus of a great organization. Everywhere on the work are evidences of the standard practice developed by engineers on other undertakings and adapted to local conditions. Without these years of preliminary engineering training, the Panama Canal as built would have been impossible.

The management of the enterprise was first placed in the hands of engineers and others who had been eminently successful in great works conducted by private capital. They were undoubtedly able men and contributed enormously to the primary work, and are deserving of great credit. They had not had experience in conducting work under the many restrictions imposed by the government, and in dealing with superiors who were representatives, not of capital and business, but of the people of the

United States. The large body of engineers in the employ of the United States were at first passed over when the greatest and most responsible engineering positions ever at the disposal of the government were to be filled. They had devoted their lives to the service and were now ignored. After but a short interval a change came, and the management was turned over to government engineers. The selections were made from the oldest, and, as a body, the most experienced, organization of engineers in the government service, the Corps of Engineers of the United States Army, and to a lesser extent, from the Corps of Civil Engineers of the United States Navy. The results of the work are a sufficient tribute to the wisdom of the selection.

The evidence is clear that a strong national sentiment pervades the force, which lends inspiration to self-sacrificing cooperation, to hard work, and to contentment under discomforts—a sentiment intensified through isolation in a foreign land. It finds expression not only in the canal employee, but in every American who admires and looks up to his fellow citizen who has worked on the canal. This element of success is fundamental, and rarely has an enterprise given so good an opportunity for its display. It might easily have been smothered by ill-advised administration, but the organization is blessed with a leader who says that "we" are building the canal, and whose inspiration leads all to take the same view. It is remarkable to note the extent to which a feeling of loyalty to the work exists, rather than to the individual or to any division. Even a company agent resident on the Isthmus, in referring to the Pacific Division, states that "We put in 4500 cubic yards of concrete on the locks yesterday." This general feeling of loyalty in no way excludes a healthful rivalry for each crew or division to excel. The individual who would ordinarily be disgruntled or dissatisfied soon leaves the Isthmus, or he finds those feelings pushed into the background or smothered by the all-pervading spirit of loyalty to the work. The whole is an interesting psychological problem, which only a visit to the Isthmus can disclose in all its force.

In the valuation by the Americans of the French canal company's property, one notable item, though an intangible one, is missing—the value to us of the French experience, the lessons learned by them through years of bitter experience. Had we begun the canal as pioneers, it is of course impossible now to state what costly mistake we might have made or what untoward conditions we might have overlooked; there can be no doubt that the knowledge of what the French had done aided us in making up our minds what to do and what not to do. One of the greatest errors of the French, and one that contributed most largely to their failure, was that they did not realize until too late the magnitude of the enterprise.

In a material way the most valuable contributions to the elements of success were the well-developed state of the art of making concrete, the perfected steam-shovel, compressed-air tools and numerous other mechanical devices.

In Conclusion

There is so much of interest connected with the subject of the Panama Canal that the most difficult problem in writing a limited article about it is to decide what to omit. The organization of the forces, the system of accounting and cost-keeping, the method of civil government, the Panama Railroad, the administration of the subsistence and storekeeping divisions, the importance of the canal to the navy, and many other subjects, offer a wealth of material—sufficient for separate essays—and are well worthy of study. All branches pertaining to the execution of the work have been studied out to a point of maximum possible efficiency, and that this has been possible is largely due to the absence of hidebound precedents and to the fact that control was left to the man on the ground.

The canal will soon be completed and begin its history as an actuality. Study and statistics throw much light upon what its commercial history will be. No one may venture to predict what momentous influence it may have in war or in preventing war. Whatever may be the detailed events in which the canal may take a part, there can be no doubt that it is one more step in the westward trend of civilization. The prophecy of sixty years ago by that farseeing statesman, William H. Seward, made in a speech in the Senate, is still in remarkable process of fulfillment:

Even the discovery of this continent and its islands, and the organization of society and government upon them, grand and important as these events have been, were not conditional, preliminary and ancillary to the more sublime result now in the act of consummation, the reunion of the two civilizations, which, parting on the plains of Asia 4000 years ago, and travelling ever after in opposite directions around the world, now meet again on the coasts and islands of the Pacific Ocean. Certainly no mere human event of equal dignity and importance has ever occurred upon the earth. It will be followed by the equalization of the condition of society and the restoration of the unity of the human family. Who does not see that henceforth, every year, European commerce, European politics, European thought and activity, although actually gaining greater force, and European connections, although actually becoming more intimate, will ultimately sink in importance; while the Pacific Ocean, its shores, its islands, and the vast regions beyond, will become the chief theater of events in the world's great hereafter?

"The Navy and the Panama Canal"

3

Captain Harry S. Knapp, USN

U.S. Naval Institute *Proceedings*
(Volume 3—1913): 931–48

THE COMPLETION OF THE PANAMA CANAL is so nearly at hand that the time has seemed appropriate to the Board of Control to publish in the *Proceedings* a discussion of the effect of the canal upon the navy. In responding to their invitation to submit a paper on this subject the writer wishes at the outset to make plain that what follows represents his personal conclusions, and that he neither desires nor is authorized to speak for anybody but himself.

Because it has the widest appeal the question of how the canal will affect the strength of the navy will be considered first and at most length. To those outside of professional circles it has a more direct and personal application than any other, because upon the answer will depend the appropriations that the taxpayer must provide. The canal has been an expensive undertaking for the United States, and the people of the country, in thinking of its bearing upon the navy, naturally anticipate that its completion may considerably modify the appropriations for the upkeep of the naval establishment. Everybody is familiar in a general way with the shortening of sea routes via the Panama Canal from our Atlantic to our Pacific coast; for instance, that the direct distance from New York or Philadelphia to San Francisco is reduced from about 13,000 miles via

Magellan to about 5000 miles via Panama, or that the distance from New Orleans to San Francisco is about 9000 miles less via the canal than via Magellan. From such general and obvious knowledge it is an easy step to the conclusion that the strength of the navy with the canal may be much less than it would necessarily be without the canal; or, what amounts to the same thing, that the appropriations for the navy may be greatly reduced as soon as the canal is opened. Twice recently within a week the writer has heard members of Congress refer to this very matter, one of them saying, in effect, that the canal would increase the effectiveness of the navy two- or three-fold, while the other thought its effectiveness would be doubled. The writer, while prepared to admit that these remarks were rather an after-dinner *façon de parler* than the expression of a deliberately formed opinion, yet believes they indicate a somewhat general impression that careful study of the situation will not justify.

A prerequisite to the formation of any intelligent conclusion on this question is an understanding of the conditions that govern the strength of the navy. The ultimate, dynamic, use of the navy is to beat the enemy in war; the every-day political use of the navy in peace is to avert war by reason of its existence ready for war. Neither purpose will be served unless the navy be adequately strong in material and personnel, and unless the personnel be trained and efficient; the navy itself is responsible for trained efficiency, but the country at large, through Congress, is responsible that adequate strength be provided.

Wars do not merely happen; they usually result from the clash of some definite policies. In an attempt to fix the strength of our navy the national policies of our government that affect other countries are a prime factor to be considered. The United States has the following definite policies in its external relations: 1st, the avoidance of entangling alliances; 2d, the Monroe Doctrine; 3d, the Open Door in the Far East; 4th, Asiatic exclusion; 5th, the control and protection of the Panama Canal itself. Where any of these policies affect adversely the interests of other nations there is the possibility of friction, and where friction arises there is always the possibility of war.

The first of the policies mentioned above may be dismissed with a word, for it is distinctly one of abstention, and so is not apt to be the cause of diverse interests. Its effect is, however, that we must play a lone hand, and that is not without a bearing on the strength of the navy. The second policy was recognized in a manner by England in the Clayton-Bulwer treaty of 1850, and to a greater degree in the Hay-Pauncefote treaty of 1901. But other nations do not accept it as international law, and it is not infrequently the subject of unfriendly comment. The Monroe Doctrine may be the occasion of friction, and so of war, with European nations, and there is a possibility that it may be with Japan, or at a later day with China. The relation of the Monroe Doctrine to the navy was pointedly indicated by Mr. Secretary Meyer, when he said in effect, for his words are not before the writer, that the Monroe Doctrine is just as strong as the navy, and no stronger. The third policy is one that may cause friction with both European and Asiatic nations. The fourth concerns our relations with Asiatic nations only. The fifth Policy is a result of a duty we have assumed single-handed for manifest reasons of advantage, and we consulted no nation about it except Great Britain. It has a very direct bearing upon the strength of the navy, upon which it throws an added responsibility.

The extension of our foreign trade that is now being so urgently advocated in connection with the change of our tariff laws cannot be placed, perhaps, under the same head as the policies just mentioned. But foreign trade certainly does involve relations with foreign nations; and, as a matter of fact, commercial and trade rivalries are most fruitful causes of misunderstanding between nations.

What has just been said does not exhaust all sources of possible wars by any means, as it does not exhaust all of our external relations. Enough has been said, however, to show reasons why war is not an improbability—certainly it is a possibility—with nations in Europe and Asia. European nations will hardly attack us in force in the Pacific, nor will any nation fronting on the Pacific be apt to attack us in force in the Atlantic. We have, therefore, to anticipate the possibility of war in the Atlantic with a European nation, and in the Pacific with an Asiatic nation.

This leads us to the formulation of a policy for the strength of the navy. It should be strong enough to safeguard our interests and meet any probable attack in either ocean and not leave our interests unguarded in the other. In explanation of the last clause it may be said that a full consideration of the subject should not stop short of the possibility of a simultaneous attack in both oceans, however improbable; a war with allied nations in the Atlantic and Pacific is not impossible. It is especially the duty of men in the military branches of the government to have their eyes open to every contingency.

In considering possible antagonists in the Atlantic Great Britain may be eliminated from consideration. In the first place it would take us many years to catch up with her in material strength if we tried, and would entail an enormous expense; in the second, war would be a blow to her commercial interests and interests of supply that she can ill afford to suffer; and, in the third, we have a hostage in Canada worth many battleships. There are, moreover, powerful interests of a more sentimental nature that are yet very real. No such strong reasons exist for eliminating any other European nation from the list of possible antagonists and the formula therefore becomes, in its final and definite statement, that our navy should be strong enough to meet in the Atlantic the maritime nation of Europe next strongest to Great Britain, and in the Pacific the strongest nation in that ocean.

As affecting the strength of the navy it is well to keep in mind also the position of the United States in the two oceans. In the Atlantic, aside from the maintenance of the Monroe Doctrine, we have a great material interest in Puerto Rico, which is our own territory; and toward Cuba and Panama we have a duty in the protection of their independence. Then there is the canal itself. All of these interests are comparatively near to us, and very much nearer than is any European adversary. In the Pacific we are in a very different case. There we have Alaska, the Hawaiian Islands, Guam, the Philippines, and Tutuila, the nearest 2000 miles and the most distant 7000 miles from our coast, and some much nearer possible adversaries in that ocean than ourselves. The distance of our outlying Atlantic interests has vastly less bearing on the strength of our fleet in that ocean than has the distance of our outlying Pacific interests on the strength of the fleet in the Pacific.

If the Atlantic and Pacific were closed oceans the formula reached above for the strength of the navy would mean that in each there should be maintained a force (that may be called the Standard Atlantic Fleet and the Standard Pacific Fleet, for brevity) sufficient for the duty in that ocean, which is the Two-Ocean Standard, pure and simple.

Neither here nor elsewhere in this paper will a concrete estimate be undertaken of the strength in numbers of ships of the "standard" fleets. Such an estimate is not reached by a simple matching of ship by ship, but is influenced also by such considerations as the probable situation of the theater of war, the possibility that the assumed antagonist may not be able to have his entire strength present in that theater for political or other reasons, and the morale of the antagonist. This may not impossibly result in the conclusion that our own necessary strength *in ships* is less than that of some possible antagonists and greater than that of others. For the present purpose no such concrete estimate is necessary and it is enough to say that the strength should be "sufficient for the duty."

Without the canal the requirements are practically the same as if the Atlantic and Pacific were closed oceans. For, though the possibility exists of reinforcement in one ocean from the other, yet the long distance to be traversed by the reinforcement by whatever route, the difficulties about fueling en route, and the danger, especially to a force coming from the Pacific, of finding the enemy between the reinforcement and the body it is attempting to join, all militate so greatly against a successful issue that it would be imprudent to count upon it.

With the canal in operation, however, a different situation arises. The route of the reinforcements will be shortened from 8000 to 10,000 miles by the canal, and that route will lie on interior lines. Fuel can be taken at stations under our own flag, separated by distances less than those representing the sea endurance of the fleet; the embarrassment arising from the necessity of avoiding any semblance of violating neutrality in fueling will thus be avoided. Junction is possible from 40 to 60 days sooner, and the enemy need not be passed to effect it. Put in another way: Guantanamo is at practically the same distance from the English Channel that it is from San Francisco via the canal; or again, the nearest Asiatic port to Honolulu is only about 1250 miles nearer than Panama, but is about 8700 miles nearer to Honolulu than our nearest Caribbean port by way of Magellan. In the face of such facts it would be difficult to maintain that the canal will have no effect on the strength of the navy, for that would be tantamount to the claim that the canal has no military value to the United States.

On the other hand, the claim that the canal will double the effectiveness of the navy or more is a great exaggeration. Though such statements probably result from loose use of language rather than a careful study of the situation, they are dangerous, for they are apt to be taken literally by the layman, and the navy cannot afford to have such an impression gain ground. To show their fallacy it is only necessary to consider the matter of distances. It is quite true that the canal will enable the fleet to be transferred from one ocean to the other in a few hours, but that is only the beginning of the problem. The added strength that the canal will give to the navy must be measured by the facility the canal affords in enabling reinforcements to arrive *in time to be of use tactically*; that is, as a part of the entire force in battle with the enemy. The canal will be of little use if the reinforcements arrive so late that the battle has already been won by the enemy. The Atlantic terminal is about 700 miles from Guantanamo, 1200 miles front the most distant part of the Caribbean, and 2000 miles from New York, no inconsiderable distances in themselves. On the Pacific side the condition is very much less favorable, for the Pacific terminal is about 3250 miles from San Francisco, 4700 from Honolulu, 8000 from Guam, and 9350 from Manila. Merely to be able to get the fleet rapidly from one ocean to another is a great gain, a very great gain; but it is not by any means the whole problem. Allowing the fleet an average speed of 12 knots from departure to destination, which is high, considering the time necessary to coal and effect repairs and the necessity that all the fighting components arrive together and *ready for action*, this means that, from the time of leaving the canal until it arrived where it would probably be needed, the shortest interval is about 58 hours to Guantanamo, and the longest is about 33 days to Manila, during which the enemy will not have been idle. The canal will be a great military asset in war, and an equally great one in anticipation of war; but it is quite beside the mark to say it will double the effectiveness of the navy, or do anything approaching that.

The truth, as usual, lies between these two extreme views just examined, and the writer believes that the former is much nearer the truth than the latter. By its very nature the problem of determining just what will be the effect of the canal upon the strength of the navy cannot be mathematically demonstrated. The solution is largely one of opinion, and will be modified as greater or less weight is given to the several considerations on which it is based. If the general formula advanced above for fixing the strength of the navy be accepted, then manifestly, canal or no canal, the minimum permissible strength of the navy is that which will enable us to meet, with our entire force, our strongest probable enemy, wherever situated. Under the same conditions the maximum strength that can be claimed as necessary is the sum of that of the Standard Atlantic Fleet plus that of the Standard Pacific Fleet (Great Britain being excluded for reasons above given). This amounts to saying that the maximum strength that can be claimed as necessary is that which will enable us to conduct a war with prospect of success in both oceans at once, which is the Two-Ocean Standard again. If the possible antagonists in the two oceans, in relation to whom our formula for strength is founded, were equally strong, our minimum permissible navy would be half as strong as the maximum navy that will ever be necessary. They are not equally strong, however, and our Standard Atlantic Fleet should now, and the condition is probably permanent, be stronger than the Standard Pacific Fleet need be. The

Standard Atlantic Fleet, therefore, is the measure of our minimum permissible strength; and, to avoid any misunderstanding, the words "minimum permissible strength" are used in the narrow sense of indicating the very least strength that can logically be believed allowable by anybody who believes in a navy at all for well-founded reasons. The quoted words do not represent the writer's views of what our minimum naval strength should be.

Our total naval strength at this minute is not equal to that of what is called above the Standard Atlantic Fleet. Hence the completion of the canal should have no immediate effect upon our building. It remains to find an answer to the question what effect will it have upon our building policy for the future?

The writer's personal opinion is that, when the canal is finished, our policy should be to have eventually, and as soon as possible, a total strength not less than that of the Standard Atlantic Fleet plus three-quarters that of the Standard Pacific Fleet. These so-called "standard" fleets are not fixed quantities, but will vary from year to year as foreign nations increase their own naval strength. The policy itself can, however, be fixed, and some policy should be established.

The reasons that have appealed to the writer in reaching this conclusion are as follows:

(a) With no canal our total strength should be the sum of both the Standard Atlantic Fleet and the Standard Pacific Fleet.

(b) The canal so greatly shortens distances between the two oceans that some reduction of strength below that of (a) is justifiable when it shall be finished, in view of the great financial burden imposed by a great navy, and the rather remote possibility of simultaneous war in both oceans.

(c) This reduction should not be sufficient to leave the nation in a hopeless case in either ocean if war broke out there while war was being waged in the other.

(d) As the strength of the Standard Atlantic Fleet must be maintained in any event, the Pacific Fleet is the one in which to make
the reduction in strength.

(e) Our interests are so great, and are scattered over such immense
distances in the Pacific, that anything less than three-quarters of
the Standard Pacific Fleet would make even a defensive war in
that ocean hopeless.

(f) With three-quarters of the Standard Pacific Fleet a defensive war,
a containing war so to speak, would not be hopeless while waging a war on equal terms in the Atlantic.

(g) If there were no prospect of war in the Pacific at a time when
engaged in war in the Atlantic, then one-half of the Standard
Pacific Fleet, and perhaps less, would suffice to guard our interests in the Pacific, leaving the rest of the fleet in that ocean free
to reinforce the Atlantic Fleet and give in the Atlantic a marked
superiority of force.

(h) If at war in the Pacific with no prospect of war in the Atlantic, a
great superiority of force could be maintained in the Pacific that
would be the more valuable, owing to the distances over which
the navy would have to operate in that ocean.

The composition of the fleet will be little affected by the existence
of the finished canal. All classes of fighting ships will be as much needed
after the canal as before, and their numbers and proportions deemed
requisite for the duty in either ocean will be necessary, canal or no canal.
It is not improbable that the defense of the canal itself may demand a
limited number of certain classes of vessels that would not otherwise be
necessary. But in its large aspect the composition of the fighting fleet can
hardly be affected by the completion of the canal. Even in the matter of
auxiliaries the same thing appears to be true. If the navy depended upon
its own auxiliaries for the transfer of supplies and fuel from one ocean
to the other, the canal would naturally serve to diminish the number of

supply and fuel ships; but such cargoes are practically all sent by contract. Other auxiliaries are based in number on the fighting ships they have to serve, and distance has little to do with the question. Speaking in a broad way, then, the existence of the canal will have no effect on the composition of the fleet.

It is more than probable that the completion of the canal will effect some changes in the disposition of the fleet in time of peace. It has already been pointed out that the navy is not now as strong as is theoretically necessary in the Atlantic alone; so that for a considerable time to come, whatever building program may be adopted, it will be necessary to concentrate our entire fighting fleet in time of war, trusting to Providence that the part sent to the threatened ocean will not be needed during the war in the ocean from which it is withdrawn. In effecting this concentration the canal will be a very great military advantage to us. In time of peace, however, the completion of the canal will enable some changes to be made in the present disposition of the fleet. The disposition now, while dictated by reasons of convenience under present-day conditions, is yet not very logical considered in the light of all-round preparedness for war. A very possible outcome will be the maintenance of a force of fixed strength in each ocean, with a shifting squadron that will go first into one and then into the other. This can be so managed as to keep in both oceans a force better balanced in all its components of fighting strength than is now the case with either. There will be other advantages also, one being the appearance on the Pacific coast of parts of the navy that cannot now be seen there. The people on the Pacific coast are as vitally interested in the navy as are those in the East; yet they habitually see the least powerful and least modern of our ships. It is natural and, indeed, commendable, that they should wish to have in their own waters at one time or another the flower of the navy. The completion of the canal will enable this to be done; and it will, further, be good policy for the navy to do it, and so stimulate the friendly interest in the navy that is always in evidence on the Pacific coast.

Another advantage that will accrue in connection with the transfer of ships from one ocean to another is the possibility of making between our own ports, and without taxing the hospitality of foreign nations, the long voyages in fleet that we believe in our service to be so advantageous as a means of fleet discipline and fleet preparedness. The entire battle fleet could easily go from New York to Seattle, stay ten days at San Francisco and ten in Puget Sound, and be back in New York in a little more than three months. As a long-distance cruise this would have many advantages over a cruise to Europe and back, not the least of which would be the experience gained in logistics over a route that the fleet may have to make some day in one direction or the other when the errand is not peaceful.

The completion of the canal will be advantageous to the navy in still another way connected with the disposition of the ships of the fleet. Corinto, Nicaragua, is less than 50 miles further distant from New York via Panama than it is from San Francisco. All the Pacific coast of Central America outside of Mexico is 1,000 miles or more nearer Panama than it is to San Francisco. It will therefore be possible generally to send ships more quickly from the Atlantic to the Pacific coast of Central America in times of disturbance there than it will be to send them from San Francisco.

The preponderance of our naval strength will probably continue to be in the future, as it has been in the past, habitually kept in the Atlantic. That ocean is the better one for the upkeep, drill and administration of the battle fleet for many reasons. But the canal will permit of many changes of disposition, some of them permanent and some temporary, that will be advantageous and that are impracticable under present conditions.

The completion of the canal should serve to bring home to everyone the importance of our naval bases in the West Indies and the Pacific. That their importance has not been adequately realized is evidenced by the lack of funds provided to put them in an efficient condition. The Monroe Doctrine was an old story before the war of 1898; but few people realized that it extended our military frontier beyond the Atlantic and Gulf coasts, for it is a mental conception and not a tangible thing appealing to the senses.

After 1898 and the acquisition of Puerto Rico there was a visible projection of our frontier into the Caribbean; and after the Hay-Pauncefote treaty in 1901, which gave the United States undivided responsibility for the canal, another visible and material interest appeared still further to the front. It has always been clear to the naval mind that our military frontier extends far beyond our continental borders, and now, irrespective of the Monroe Doctrine, it extends from the Atlantic coast around Puerto Rico to the canal; and it has been equally clear that, for the security of that frontier, a naval base somewhere on the outer edge of the Caribbean is a necessity. After careful consideration Guantanamo was selected as the site for such a base as being the suitable harbor situated furthest to the front on the edge of the Caribbean. Congress has not yet recognized its appreciation of the necessity for Guantanamo by the provision of an adequate program for its defense and equipment, though there are some signs of such an appreciation. Nor do the people of some of the gulf states realize that the frontier has advanced more than a thousand miles from their coast, and that the New Orleans and Pensacola naval stations no longer serve any useful military purpose, if one may judge by their arguments against the action of the Navy Department in closing them during the last administration. When the canal becomes a great utility in regular operation instead of an interesting engineering work, when trade has settled into the new routes the canal will make possible and when business men have occasion to think of it daily as a vital link in their transportation problems, a juster appreciation will arise of the necessity of a naval base at Guantanamo for the protection of the canal and of the trade routes converging toward it, as well as for the maintenance of our general interests in the Caribbean, that will doubtless find expression in a complete scheme for its defense and equipment.

If, as it almost surely will, the canal serves to place in the Pacific Ocean, even for a part of the time only, a greater force and one of larger ships than is now kept there, the question of bases in that ocean must be considered. In the Pacific, excepting our limited plant in the Philippines, there are three bases—Mare Island, Bremerton, and Pearl Harbor. To care for any considerable force in peace, and, what is more important, to care for it in war, these are all too few. Pearl Harbor is in the making, and Bremerton is not yet a first-class base. San Francisco Bay is the place above all others on our Pacific continental coast that is suited for a naval base by reason of its strategic situation geographically and the advantages attending the proximity of a large city. But the Mare Island Navy Yard is impossibly situated for this purpose. It has neither the area nor the depth of water needed for modern capital ships and its distance from San Francisco and lack of a railway connection are handicaps in the supply of labor and in the economical handling of freight and building supplies. At the present time the available depth is 22 feet at mean lower low water, and the channels constantly and rapidly silt up. It is even difficult to keep the entrance to the new dry-dock deep enough for safe docking of ships that can enter it. The adopted departmental policy is to have 40 feet depth from the sea to our navy yards, and that depth of channel is being urged at our important commercial ports in the interests of commerce. To all except those who will not see, it has been increasingly evident during the last ten years that the Mare Island Navy Yard is doomed for the service of modern capital ships, and it is equally evident that a new location, somewhere in San Francisco Bay, on deep water near the city, must eventually, be provided for their docking and repair. If the people of California desire and expect to see any considerable part of our modern fleet habitually visiting in their waters after the canal is finished, they cannot too soon bestir themselves to provide in the deep water of San Francisco Bay the naval facilities that are required for the supply, upkeep and repair of modern capital ships. Mare Island does not afford them, for the simple reason that recent capital ships cannot safely go there, if for no other. Men cannot drive rivets on a ship 20 to 30 miles away. The completion of the canal should help to force this conclusion home if the people of California are not prepared to accept it now.

Of Pearl Harbor and Bremerton there is less occasion to speak in this connection. Congress is treating Pearl Harbor in a liberal spirit, and the facilities at Bremerton are gradually increasing. The development of both should go on to provide for the increased naval shipping that may naturally be expected to follow the completion of the canal; but, above all, to provide for the greatly increased demand upon them in the event of a war in the Pacific.

The consideration that perhaps comes most naturally to mind in connection with the canal is the immense shortening of distances effected by it in most cases between points in the Atlantic and Pacific. This consideration was, of course, the reason for building it. What may be termed the commercial routes from New York to Hong Kong, those that take in ports of call, are practically the same length via Panama and Suez, the difference between them being less than 20 miles in favor of Suez; but the Panama route is the shorter from New York to Shanghai and the ports of Japan. From New York to Manila the Panama route is shorter than that by Suez unless the former go by way of Honolulu and Yokohama. The further east the point in the Pacific, the greater the gain in distance to New York by the Panama route. Valparaiso is 3750 miles nearer New York via Panama than via Magellan. Speaking generally, the distance is shortened via the canal from New York to any point in the Pacific inside of a line drawn from Magellan Strait, through Australia and the Philippines, to Hong Kong. As affecting naval movements this means more than time and fuel saved, though both economies are of prime importance. It means the possibility of sending ships from the Atlantic to almost any place where they will be needed in the Pacific by a route that has fuel stations under our flag along the entire distance, no two of which are further apart than the fuel endurance of our capital ships. This is an enormous advantage, for the problem of fueling our naval ships in time of war on a passage from the Pacific to the Atlantic, or vice versa, would be a staggering one by either the Suez or Magellan route, and the attitude of neutrals might make it almost an unsolvable one. The canal will eliminate the question of neutrality altogether, and for that reason alone it is of incalculable benefit to the navy.

The question of economy is, however, one not to be ignored. Between New York and San Francisco, in either direction, Panama and Guantanamo would probably be ports of call for a fleet. A study of the saving of time, fuel and money effected by sending a fleet between Panama and Guantanamo through the canal instead of through Magellan gives some astonishing results. Such a study has been made, based on the movement of 25 capital ships with attendant cruisers, destroyers and auxiliaries. It is too long to give more than the results, but they are sufficiently interesting.

The time saved under the assumptions is about 60 days. This could be considerably shortened by increasing the assumed sea speed, or decreasing the days at anchor for coaling, repairs, and recuperation of the personnel, but at the expense of fuel burned, with the attendant cost and necessity of fueling oftener. The route via Magellan that the fleet would follow between Guantanamo and Panama requires nearly 900 actual steaming hours at 12 knots, or 37 days. This makes no allowance for necessary time to refuel and repair, so that 60 days is not an unreasonable gain in time to allow in favor of the canal, in view of the fact that refueling on the Magellan route would have to be carried on at places outside the territorial limits of neutrals, and often under disadvantageous circumstances. This might be time enough to enable the enemy to finish the campaign in his favor, not to speak of the harassment of the personnel while making the long sea voyage via Magellan, during which every man would know that he and his ship were needed every moment of the time, with the prospect that the fleet would not arrive after all in time to effect its purpose.

The saving in coal is about 290,000 tons, and in fuel oil about 54,000 tons. At the present market values of these fuels taken for the conditions, this means a money saving of nearly $3,000,000. Not to overestimate this saving, and assuming that an oversupply of 20 per cent has been allowed, the saving in coal would still be 240,000 tons, in oil 45,000 tons, and in money $2,500,000.

The gain in time is the all-important economy, but the saving in money is itself important. In view of our lack of a merchant marine, however, the simplification in the supply of fuel via the canal is of vastly greater moment than the money saving. The United States can furnish whatever money the circumstances of war may demand, but it cannot build over-night a merchant marine for the service of the fleet. This subject could be greatly elaborated, but enough has been said to show what a valuable military asset the canal is in its bearing on fleet logistics.

Simply for the ordinary service of the fleet in time of peace the canal will effect very large savings to the naval appropriations. A fair average price for eastern coal of a kind fit for naval use is $8.45 per ton at San Francisco, Puget Sound and Honolulu. While no exact prediction can be made, competent authorities believe that, when the canal is in operation, the price at which eastern coals can be laid down at these places will be not more than $6.20 per ton. Taking as a basis the amount of coal on naval account sent to the Pacific in the last fiscal year, 160,000 tons, the saving amounts to $360,000. Nor does the advantage end there; a collier can take a cargo via the canal to the Pacific coast, discharge and be back at Norfolk in the time she would take to make the voyage out via Magellan. This roughly divides by two the tonnage necessary for any given supply of coal at those ports. In time of war in the Pacific, this will be of inestimable advantage, considering our woeful lack of a merchant marine. With respect to other bulky naval supplies, like provisions, the same thing does not hold true, for they can be delivered equally well and at little difference in cost on either coast from their points of origin. Even ammunition and guns, which are practically all manufactured in the east, would very probably be sent by rail to the Pacific in order to save time, though the expense would be greater. But with oil fuel, again, the advantage to the navy is apparent, and this time the gain is in movement toward the Atlantic. In the last few months the price of oil has markedly increased. California produces more oil than any other state and its price is lower than eastern oils. This fact, in addition to the important fact that a large oil-producing area has been set aside for naval purposes in California, points to the possibility that the navy may soon be using California oil in the Atlantic, which would hardly be possible without the canal. The demand for oil increases every day and many of the older wells are falling off in production; the navy may not improbably have great occasion in the years to come to congratulate itself that the canal will make the Pacific coast fields available.

Modifications of trade routes that will follow the completion of the canal are sure eventually to cause a reduction in freight rates, and so act as a stimulus to trade. The increased trade will, in turn, demand a greater tonnage, though this demand will be partially met at first by the ability of the same amount of shipping to provide for a greater trade because of the shortened distances via the canal. Still it can hardly be doubted that the opening of the canal will create a demand in time for an amount of shipping considerably greater than exists now in order to provide for the increased trade. The opinion has been advanced that the United States merchant marine will be greatly stimulated by the operation of these causes. The navy earnestly hopes that this may be true, for a large merchant marine is a necessity for a strong navy only in a less degree than the auxiliary ships especially designed for its service; and anything whatever that can properly be done to increase the merchant marine should have the active support of the navy. In so far as the coasting trade is concerned there seems to be good reason to expect an increase of United States shipping, for that trade is certain to grow rapidly upon the opening of the canal, and foreigners cannot take any part in it. Moreover, the exemption of this class of shipping from the payment of canal tolls will virtually be a subsidy. Already some ships have been built for this trade in anticipation of the completion of the canal, and others are being built. But the writer has been unable to convince himself that the opening of the canal will alone serve to draw American capital into a form of investment from which it has persistently kept aloof, and under present conditions and laws he anticipates little or no resultant increase in that part of the merchant marine of the United States engaged in foreign trade. Without any close examination of the reason why, it seems to be a fact that Americans either cannot or else do not care to compete with other maritime nations in the sea carriage of foreign trade, and it is not apparent that the opening of the canal will by itself change that condition. That we should have a flourishing merchant marine is a matter of such vital interest to the navy that it will anticipate with satisfaction the increase of shipping engaged in coastwise trade due to the opening of the canal; and, as remarked above, the navy should exert its influence in favor of every proper measure tending to put American ships on the ocean in the foreign trade.

However interesting and profitable it may be to dwell upon the military advantages to the United States attending the opening of the canal, that feature is not the most vital one to the navy. The canal puts an added and very great responsibility upon the navy, and this fact is one that the navy and its friends must always keep in mind.

The canal is being built, and it will be operated and controlled, solely by the United States government. The protection of the canal, therefore, falls solely upon the United States. Moreover, in the Hay-Pauncefote treaty of 1901, the neutralization rules are embodied in Article 3, in which the language is: "The United States adopts, as the basis of the neutralization of such ship canal, the following rules. . . ." We are, therefore, the sole guarantors of the neutralization of the canal. Again Article I of the treaty of November 18, 1903, with Panama reads: "The United States guarantees and will maintain the independence of the Republic of Panama." Finally, the United States trade passing through the canal will be very great. Here are new and great responsibilities, all flowing from the canal, and all dependent upon the navy for their realization. The navy is the outer line of defense of the canal as it is of the country. The inner line of defense of the canal resides in the fortifications and garrison at the canal itself. If our navy is driven from the sea and made negligible, an enemy with a great army can undertake with impunity the transportation of the troops necessary to overcome the inner line of defense and complete the victory begun on the ocean. The task may not be easy for him, but its possibility must be conceded if the sea is closed to us and open to the enemy. The only possible and final assurance of safety for the canal is in a navy strong enough to meet the enemy, beat him, and prevent him from ever getting near it. The following words, quoted from Admiral Mahan, indicate the alternative: "Permanent [naval] inferiority means inevitably ultimate defeat, which fortifications can only delay." And a few lines later he uses these words: "If the United States desires peace with security, it must have a navy second to none but that of Great Britain; to rival which is inexpedient, because for many reasons unnecessary."

The United States is not a military nation. There is little consideration and less understanding among the people at large of military matters. The government has no defined military policy, using "military" in its wide sense, and it has no defined naval policy. By this is meant that there is no soberly thought-out relation between our military strength and our situation in the world—between our declared external political policies and the only means yet found efficacious to uphold them—that manifests itself as a guiding principle in Congress, or even in the recommendations to Congress. There should be such a military policy, and it should carry on from administration to administration, from Congress to Congress, and be considered a part of our foreign affairs policy, as little open to attack from within our own household as the external policies on which it is founded. Our form of government, the immensity of our country, and our isolated position, almost insular as far as other first-class nations having great military strength are concerned, all doubtless conspire to cause the general lack of interest of our people in foreign affairs, which is the ultimate cause why there is so little appreciation of the underlying need for a strong navy. The navy is popular just now, and to that degree it is fortunate; but the roots of its existence should lie in deeper ground than popularity. It is to be hoped that the completion of the canal may serve to broaden the national outlook, and that we may be able to look back to it in coming years as the period in which a reasoned national policy, founded on national aims, shall have had its birth in the country at large.

There would be no excuse for a failure of the navy itself to have a "reason for the faith that is in us"; nor can that reproach be laid at the door of the navy, which has for years had a definite, consistent policy as expressed by the responsible advisers of the Navy Department. Moreover, the effect of the canal upon that policy has been carefully kept in mind since the day the canal was started.

4 "A German View of the Strategic Importance of the Panama Canal"*

Dr. F. Zadow, Privatdozent of the
University of Greifswald

Translated by Lieutenant Commander
E. J. King, USN

U.S. Naval Institute *Proceedings*
(Volume 3—1914): 803–7

TRANSLATOR'S NOTE: *The author first gives a brief history of
the proposals for a canal and the attempts to construct one. He then
takes up the economic importance of the Canal, pointing out that
its economic value is greatest for trade bound to and from the west
coasts of South and North America, from and to European and
eastern United States ports, and that it is most of value to the United States in this respect. He remarks that England and Germany
must keep a careful lookout in order that they may get their shares
of the trade which is to pass through this new international highway. He concludes this part of his article with the characteristic
German expression "Deutschland sei wach" (Germany on guard!).
He then takes up the strategic importance of the Canal in the following manner.*

THE POLITICAL IMPORTANCE of the Panama Canal is greater than its
economic value; it was not built primarily as a trade route but as an instrument of war. Without the Canal the United States could only arrange

---

* Extracted and translated from an article entitled "The Economic
and Strategic Importance of the Panama Canal," appearing in
Ueberall (Berlin) for February, 1914.

for adequate protection to both its Atlantic and Pacific coasts by means of two fleets; upon the completion of the Canal a transfer of the one fleet or of a part of it from the one ocean to the other will be a matter of but a few hours, whereas formerly it took many weeks. The United States also saves the enormous expense of constructing a second battle-fleet, in which must be included the saving in fuel, stores, personnel, and the cost of up-keep.

Of course the Panama Canal will retain its strategic importance only as long as it has no rivals. If, for example, any other power were to build the Darien Canal or the Nicaraguan Canal and make it secure in a military and political sense, the importance of the Panama Canal in international affairs would be materially lessened, as the United States could not then control the passage from ocean to ocean of the war- and trade-fleets of the interested nations. The possession of such a canal by a foreign power would enable an enemy fleet to effect the change from one ocean to the other without either the knowledge or the consent of the United States and would afford to their opponents the means whereby to effect a surprise and to compel the United States to divide its forces. However, the completion of the Panama Canal itself should definitely put an end to all possibilities in the shape of rival canals.

A similar effect could be produced by the simultaneous attack of two large co-operating fleets, one in the Atlantic and one in the Pacific, even when the Panama Canal is the only one in existence. It is for this reason that the English-Japanese as well as the Russo-Japanese alliance is of such unpleasant importance to the United States, for both alliances are suitable, in case of war, to bring into question the strategic value of the Panama Canal, by means of joint action of the allied fleets. Hence the endeavors of United States foreign policy to effect arbitration treaties with England and with Russia without depending solely upon racial dissimilarities to make the alliances of merely nominal worth.

From the foregoing premises it may be clearly seen that in strategical considerations lies the importance, to the United States, of those countries

(Mexico, Central America, Colombia) in whose territories it is possible to construct canals; with these considerations in mind, the political happenings in those countries are better understood. Thus may be explained the revolt of Panama from Colombia; the next to the last insurrection in Mexico, which occurred when that country wished to enter into an alliance with Japan; the efforts made by the United States to prevent the yellow races from obtaining a foothold in these countries; and finally, the persistent endeavor of the United States to extend the Monroe Doctrine* to include Central and South America.

In recognition of the fact that strategical superiority can only be maintained while the United States not only controls the Panama Canal politically but while it is defended against sudden attack by sea, the Canal is protected on both coasts by extraordinarily strong fortifications of the most modern design.

As far as distances enter into consideration there may be cited the following strategical data:

1. From San Francisco the Pacific fleet commands the entire coasts of America and the islands adjacent to the coasts; but of the oceanic islands it commands only the Hawaiian group; the remainder of the Pacific Ocean lies within the sphere of control of Japan.

2. Without the Panama Canal the Atlantic fleet, proceeding around South America, could only get as far as Valparaiso before the Japanese could reach the same point.

3. After the Panama Canal is opened the Atlantic fleet will command South and North America as far north as San Francisco and could join the Pacific fleet there unharmed. The Atlantic fleet is nearer to Central and South America than is the Pacific fleet.

---

* TRANSLATOR'S NOTE: Germany has never acknowledged the Monroe Doctrine; it is apparently not any too well understood in Germany, even in those quarters where it should be thoroughly comprehended.

From the foregoing data it is evident that the completion of the Panama Canal will furnish the United States with an important increase of strength on its west front, *i.e.,* towards Japan. Had Japan been thinking seriously of war with the United States she should not have waited until the time of the opening of the Panama Canal. It is not a sufficient answer to say that the Japanese fleet would be so much stronger at the time the first American man-of-war traverses the new waterway that it could then encounter the United States on more even terms. The fact is that Japan, with her overmastering desire for expansion, has suffered a severe setback through the opening of the Panama Canal.

From the obvious strategic considerations it is also manifest that the influence of the United States on the republics of South America will increase, as they will become, on account of the Canal, politically more dependent on the United States, *e.g.,* the case of Colombia, which, without a canal of her own and without allies, either must have two fleets or must remain assailable on two sides, and therefore is more dependent than before the opening of the Canal. It will depend largely upon the skill of the diplomats and financiers of the United States whether Colombia, the possessor of the Isthmus of Darien, organizes a political union of the nature of a "Latin Confederacy," composed of the adjacent states, or merely organizes them economically against the United States.

The Panama Canal is also important to the entire Pacific Ocean lying beyond the American continents and especially so to the colonial possessions of the United States. The Americans will become, in a military sense, independent with respect to the Philippine Islands, which are of such paramount importance for naval bases, coaling stations, cable stations, etc. Although the Samoan Islands are only of moderate strategic importance, the Hawaiian Islands comprise the principal station on lines of operations leading towards Asia and Australia. The possession of the Hawaiian Islands is equivalent to mastery of the Pacific. The United States is now establishing on the island of Oahu a fleet-base (Pearl Harbor) of extraordinary strength and importance; the first blow of Japan would apparently fall on this base. As the distance from New York to Pearl Harbor is reduced from 13,280 miles via the Straits of Magellan to 6726 miles via the Panama Canal, it is evident that the position of the United States is materially strengthened in the Pacific.

In the event of war between the United States and European powers the Panama Canal will not be of great strategic importance, as in such case—because of the importance of the east coast of the United States—the decision will take place in the Atlantic. In the case of a common goal in the Indian Ocean or in eastern Asia a fleet going out from Europe via the Suez Canal would have a material advantage; the route via the Cape of Good Hope is also more favorable for European countries, as they have colonies and bases en route which the United States wholly lacks. On the other hand, the harbors of the British colonies of Australia and New Zealand will be brought much nearer to the center of power of the United States than to the mother country, a situation that will not facilitate British policy in the Pacific. It should be remembered that England can, in case of war, and in spite of all declarations of neutrality, use her own judgment to deny use of the Suez Canal and thus monopolize the traffic through it for her own sea-borne trade; the Panama Canal now changes England's commanding position in respect of world traffic in that it affords to other countries a second highway to the Far East, and one that is not under British control. Because of the Panama Canal, England's influence, hitherto paramount throughout the world, will be decreased in the first instance and in a geographical sense with respect to the eastern shores of the Pacific Ocean and in the South Seas; however, her command of the sea in other parts of the world will not be affected, as she possesses strong strategic positions; on the one hand, along the Suez Canal route and in Africa and eastern Asia, and on the other hand, in Canada and in West Indian waters.

Inasmuch as the high-tensioned economic rivalry of nations inevitably brings war into play to render the final decision, sooner or later there must come, as nearly as human judgment can predict, a decisive conflict in the Pacific. It is certain that the extraordinary strengthening of the strategic position of the United States, and of the maritime power thereby created, in immediate proximity to the Japanese Empire, presents an obvious war danger which is openly prepared for in the United States, while in Japan the preparations are secret. Thus it is seen that the Panama Canal which, following the conquest of the Philippines, indicates the progress of the United States in carrying out its present-day paramount, imperialistic policies, will soon be the cause of a tremendous conflict, and of the resultant decision.

"Shall We Outgrow the Panama Canal?"

5

Lieutenant Commander P. V. H. Weems, USN

U.S. Naval Institute *Proceedings*
(January 1924): 7–13

IT IS ONLY RECENTLY THAT the Panama Canal has begun to operate under normal conditions, free from the effects of the World War, and with the slides sufficiently under control to make the operation of the canal continuous. The canal tolls for the fiscal year ending June 30, 1922, amounted to $11,197,832 while the cost of operation was $7,407,998, leaving a net revenue of $3,789,834. Since the present canal commenced to yield a revenue over and above the cost of operation, suggestions have been made by various parties that another canal be dug across the Nicaragua route. While there are arguments in favor of another canal, the need is so remote that the undertaking of another canal at this time would be a poor investment.

It is good business for a manufacturing concern to have the manufacturing facilities expand in proportion to the demand for the articles produced, but it would be poor policy to double these facilities years before the capacity of the original plant is reached. In other words the plant should grow in proportion to the required output and not so far in advance of it as to make the business a poor investment. In the case of the Panama Canal we have only about twenty-five per cent of the possible capacity utilized, yet there is considerable agitation for the construction of another canal doubling the ultimate capacity of the present canal. If we could worry along without any sort of canal until 1914, it seems that we should be able to get along with the greatest canal in the world at least thirty or forty years. Especially is this true when it is known that the possible capacity via the Panama Canal is something like 50,000,000 net tons per year.

Granting that several years would be required for the construction of the Nicaraguan Canal, yet if the capacity of the Panama Canal should be reached in the near future it would mean such a business boom that we could well afford to push the construction of a new canal to the limit regardless of the cost of the work.

This, no doubt, would cut the time of construction below the original estimate, and would embarrass shipping only a few years if at all. It is far better to invest the relatively small sum in increasing the capacity of the present canal before we undertake the tremendous task of building a new canal.

Some of the principal advantages of a Nicaraguan canal would be: (1) The amount of traffic could be doubled provided there is sufficient shipping; (2) The military advantage of having two routes; (3) Shorter distances via the new route; (4) Preventing any other country from undertaking the construction of such a canal. The principal argument against the canal are the first cost and the fact that the capacity of the present canal can be increased four-fold at relatively small cost. At present about 12,000,000 net tons of shipping pass through the Panama Canal each year. The traffic is handled between 7:00 A.M. and about 10:00 P.M. By continuous operation for the entire twenty-four hours the transits would be increased a proportionate amount. After the capacity of the canal has been reached in regard to the physical operation of handling the traffic, the number of transits might be limited during the dry season to the available water supply. The water from Gatun lake is distributed approximately as follows: fifty per cent through Gatun spill-way; twenty-five per cent for hydro-electric power; eleven per cent to evaporation on the lake surface—164 square miles; eleven per cent for lockages, and three per cent for municipal and other purposes. These figures vary from year to year depending on the run-off and the number of transits through the canal. Either by saving more of the water which is wasted over the spill-way, or by restricting the amount of water employed for hydro-electric purposes, the amount of water for lockages can be increased. The evaporation is nearly constant from year to year, and the amount of water used for municipal and other purposes is negligible. From May to November, which is the wet season, the water supply is greater than needed. The lake is filled to the maximum level of eighty-seven feet above sea level after which the surplus water is wasted over the spill-way. A higher level than eighty-seven feet would flood the motors operating the lock gates. During the dry season, lasting from about December to April, the water supply is not sufficient to maintain the lake level at eighty-seven feet. During the dry season of 1920 the lake reached the lowest recorded level, eighty-one and seven tenths feet. The minimum level should not be less than seventy-nine feet as this would give a minimum depth in the canal of thirty-nine feet. In order to reduce the amount of water now used for generating power, fuel must be supplied to generate the power, a costly make-shift.

A comprehensive scheme is proposed whereby the greater part of the water now lost through the spill-way may be utilized for lockages. The plan is to construct across the Chagres River at Allahuela, about ten miles up the river from Gamboa, an impounding dam 157 feet high which would raise the level in the storage lake to 227 feet above the sea. The amount of water thus stored during the rainy season would be sufficient to raise the level in Gatun lake three feet, i.e., the amount of water storage would be increased about forty per cent. The estimated cost of the project is about $5,000,000. Since the discharge from the Chagres River is more than half the total water supply of the lake, such a dam would give practically full control of the water supply.

By constructing another set of locks alongside the present ones, making the locks triple instead of double ones, the capacity of the canal would be further increased by fifty per cent. It is estimated that after these proposed alterations have been made the canal can handle 50,000,000 net tons of shipping annually. At present the canal is handling about 12,000,000 net tons annually. In other words by making a comparatively small investment on the present canal, its capacity can be made to handle four times more tonnage than is now being handled. Experts estimate that these improvements will be sufficient for at least thirty years, after which the canal might be outgrown.

Thirty years is a mighty long time. By 1953 air routes may be in competition with the water routes. At any rate any calculations made for thirty years hence have an excellent chance of being thrown out by changing conditions. Even supposing that the canal should draw more shipping than it could handle, the inexorable law of supply and demand could be utilized, and the amount of shipping decreased by increasing the tolls. It would be almost beyond all expectations to have the maximum number of ships sent through the canal with the toll rates raised, say twenty-five per cent.

After considering these points it would seem more logical to hold full rights in Nicaragua, but to postpone actual construction of another canal until its need is clearly seen. The reduction in the distances via the Nicaragua route would be comparatively small. The military advantage is an important consideration yet with a small portion of the amount necessary to build another canal, a force could be built and left on the west coast to compensate for the ships which might be cut off through the destruction of the Panama Canal. If we give due credit to General Goethals' judgment, the danger of complete destruction of the Panama Canal is not so great as some would have it. General Goethals stated that in order to put the canal completely out of commission it would be necessary for the enemy to place bombs behind the gates of the locks, and he wondered what our force would be doing in the meantime. Doubtless the destructiveness of bombs has been greatly increased since the General made this statement, yet the mere dropping of bombs in the vicinity of the locks or spill-ways would not necessarily put the canal out of commission. The solar plexus of the canal, to judge from casual observation which anyone may make who passes through the canal, would seem to be the Miraflores spillway. This could be corrected in large measure by the construction of a second dam near the present one. The construction of a second canal would entail the expense of its defense, and would give the enemy one more outlying point to attack.

From a commercial standpoint, the present canal seems to be a paying proposition. Last year a new accounting system was put into operation. The value of the canal was estimated as for any commercial concern and hereafter the financial reports will be based on the estimated valuation. The canal activities have been divided into three classes: (1) Canal transit property, (2) Canal business property, and (3) Defense capital expenditures. The value of the canal transit property was estimated to be $246,418,990; that of the canal business property, including the docks, repair shops, etc., at $28,760,308, and for defense capital expenditures $110,997,602, making a total of $386,176,900, which was the approximate cost of the canal. The amount of the canal defense expenditures might be said to be the amount the property was written down, in order to place it on a purely commercial basis.

The canal transit property was amortized on the basis of a life for fixed property as 100 years, with allowed interest at three per cent, and with the business property depreciated on the basis of its estimated life. Hereafter if the yearly report shows a revenue above the operating expenses including the annual amortization, the canal is on a sound financial basis, and in 100 years the entire value of the canal would be written off. Of course we hope for even better financial returns, and these hopes are more than justified by recent performance.

However bright the present prospect of the Panama Canal, the expenditure of $300,000,000 in the construction of another canal via the Nicaragua route would appear to be a risky adventure. Let us wait for the day when the capacity of the present canal is reached before we undertake the construction of another canal. By canceling a few "ifs" we would not have the present canal; therefore it seems that we should try to be satisfied, for at least a little while, with what is easily the greatest canal since the world began.

Comment and Discussion on "Shall We Outgrow the Panama Canal?"

6

Captain A. W. Hinds, USN

U.S. Naval Institute *Proceedings*
(February 1924): 248–52

CAPTAIN A. W. HINDS, U.S. NAVY.—I read Mr. Weems' paper with a great deal of interest and I am in agreement with him that the government should not dig another canal connecting the Atlantic and Pacific oceans until the second great ditch is needed.

Soon after the present Marine Superintendent reported for duty, in April, 1923, we began to have difficulty with the steering of some of the deep draft ships in making Canal transit. The most notable trouble makers were ore ships in the Chile-New York trade and heavily laden oil tankers. Some of these drew as much as thirty-four feet in fresh water and as the lake level goes down, near the end of the dry season, the small amount of water under their keels added to the fact that these ships handle none too well any way gave us some anxiety in their transits of the narrow waters of Gaillard Cut. In looking around for the cheapest means to increase the depth in the Cut during the dry season, we were naturally led to a study of the limitations of the Canal and the increase of traffic it may be called upon to handle in the not very distant future.

The volume of traffic through the Canal is limited by:

(a) The necessity of lock overhaul;
(b) The capacity of the locks; and

(c) The capacity of the storage area for collection of water needed in lockages.

Ordinary traffic can flow through the Canal in two streams, as ships can pass even in the narrowest part of the cut, but about once in three years the lock machinery must be thoroughly overhauled. The great valves used in handling the water must be taken out and machined and their seats removed. The lock gates must be scaled and painted and their water seals replaced. Heretofore, since the pressure of traffic did not become heavy until the early part of 1923, about four months have been allowed for lock overhaul and the work has been done during daylight hours, principally with the lock-operating and maintenance personnel.

In the future, however, the steadily increasing traffic will force the Canal authorities to work night and day at the overhaul and by doing this and carefully planning to have all material ready, a set of locks can be over-hauled in about six weeks.

In order to predict the time when the Canal will reach its capacity and when various changes will be forced upon us, it becomes necessary for one to assume the dangerous role of a prophet. It seems hardly safe to base anything on Panama Canal past performances, for the transits at Panama were interfered with by slides and then the great war came to entirely dis-arrange the normal flow of sea-borne commerce.

In order to obtain some kind of a gauge to assist in predicting the increase of traffic through the Panama Canal, the increase of passages through Suez between 1880 and 1910, when unaffected by any great war, was taken as a guide. It was believed that due to the rapid increase of population on our West Coast and to the fact that there is little coal or iron on the Pacific slope, there must be a marked increase in the shipping ser-vice between our Atlantic and Pacific coasts. It was therefore thought that a very conservative estimate would be made in saying that the increase in traffic through the Panama Canal will be as great as the increase in Suez between the years of 1880 and 1910.

We then took ships per month as an ordinate and years as abscissa, and taking as a point the average ships per month passing through the Panama Canal in the first five months of 1923, we drew through this point a line parallel to the Suez increase 1880–1910 and assumed this line would show the rate of increase of traffic at Panama. The curve gave predictions for Panama passages as follows:

Year	Predicted Average, Ships per Month
1925	430
1930	540
1935	650
1940	760
1945	880
1950	990
1955	1,100
1960	1,210
1965	1,320
1970	1,430
1975	1,540
1980	1,650

When a set of locks is under overhaul about the best the Canal can do is to put through the other twin lock thirty ships a day, and it is a very safe prediction to say that when traffic is held up the Government will be forced to come to the rescue in some way, if it is possible to do so.

An inspection of the preceding table shows we shall have thirty ships a day about 1946, so by that time we must find some way to relieve the pressure during lock overhaul. There is only one way to do this and that is by building a third system of locks paralleling the double locks already in use.

When the present Canal was built there was very little attention paid to economy—the slogan was "Make the dirt fly," but by going a little more slowly the locks that will be needed in 1946 could be built far more cheaply than the original construction. Assuming that ten years is ample time to construct the additional locks in the most economical manner, it can be seen that they must be begun in 1936, only twelve years from now.

Water Storage Capacity

The water in Gatun Lake, eighty to eighty-seven feet above sea level, is used in three principal ways: (1) It reaches the Atlantic or Pacific through the locks when ships are locked through; (2) some of it is used for electric power production, passing into the Atlantic through the mill race at Gatun Dam; and (3) some of it evaporates.

The rainy season begins at Panama about May 1 and continues until about the fifteenth of December. During this period there is no worry over the water supply, and the lake level gradually rises until it is eighty-seven feet above the sea. During the latter part of the rainy season, when the rainfall is heaviest, some of the spillway gates at Gatun must be opened and the water allowed to escape, as otherwise it would overflow into the lock chambers and into the lock machinery operating spaces. Unfortunately, the locks were so designed that the water level in Gatun Lake cannot be increased in height to more than eighty-seven feet above the sea. Changes to increase this height one or two feet and thus add a big percentage to the storage volume do not seem practicable.

At the end of the wet season the lake is always at a height of eighty-seven feet above the sea, and at this time there is a depth of forty-seven feet in Gaillard Cut. As some deep draft vessels using the Canal draw as much as thirty-four feet, they have thirteen feet under their keels when the lake is at maximum height.

Soon after the fifteenth of December, when the dry season comes in, the lake level begins to fall, and when it has fallen about seven feet there are only forty feet of water in the Cut, and the deep draft vessels begin to behave badly, sheer over toward the banks, and sometimes hit them. Naval officers who have served on battleships know how difficult it is to maneuver them in shallow water. This same principle applies to a deep

draft vessel in the Cut when the lake gets low. The matter is highly specu-
lative, but the present Marine Superintendent would not like to see the
depth of water in Gaillard Cut reduced to below forty feet.

Even when carrying forty feet of water in Gaillard Cut, its actual
depth is reduced by what are called the "surges." When water is drawn
into the inshore Pacific docks it must be replaced by water from Gatun
Lake. The water must flow through the long, narrow Cut, and it is taken
so fast that the actual depth in the Cut is reduced by about a foot and a
half. It follows that with forty-foot depth in the Cut, there are practically
only thirty-eight and five-tenths feet, so a thirty-four-foot draft ship has
really only four and five-tenths feet of water under her keel. These ships
sometimes behave so badly that the pilots refer to them as "bad actors."

There are two projects in mind for carrying a little more depth in
Gaillard Cut during the dry season. The minor one of these is to build a
small lock supply reservoir at the inshore Pacific lock. This would cost
about a million dollars and would reduce the "surges" to an inapprecia-
ble amount and add, in effect, about a foot and a half to the depth in
the Cut.

The other and more ambitious project is to add to the water storage
by building a dam costing about six million dollars at Alhajuela, some
thirteen miles up the Chagres River from the Canal prism.

Both these schemes will be carried out in time, but it would be a great
addition to Canal efficiency to carry out these improvements at once.

According to water storage figures given by the Chief Hydrographer
of the Canal Government, even when the lock supply reservoir and the
Alhajuela storage dam are built, there is a water supply limit to the capacity of the Canal in ship lockages.

There is a fine morale in the Panama Canal personnel, as all hands
have been educated to guard with jealousy the reputation of this big piece
of engineering. In deriving the figures as to ultimate water supply, the
Hydrographer was therefore very conservative. He assumed that we will
again be faced with a dry season as in 1920, the longest and driest on

record, and under these assumptions he calculates that when the additional water storage is provided 1,630 lockages per month can be made and still have forty feet of water in the Cut at the end of the dry season.

A glance at the table shows that if the traffic increases at the same rate Suez traffic increased from 1880–1910 and all practicable improvements are made, we shall reach the ultimate capacity of the Panama Canal about 1979.

There should be no trouble about the wherewithal to make all the improvements noted if Congress can be induced to appropriate for Canal improvements and changes only a small portion of the money collected for tolls. The tolls are now running over two million dollars a month. If we accept the table of predicted increase in traffic and assume that the Canal Government will be run economically and the total rate not changed, the big ditch should clear an average of thirty-five million dollars a year between 1930 and 1950.

Summarizing it can be seen:

1. That we need now a small storage of water near the inshore Pacific locks to prevent the temporary reduction of depth in Gaillard Cut when the locks are being filled. In addition this will prevent currents in the Cut. The cost will be something like a million dollars.

2. That we need now the additional water storage Alhajuela dam will give in order that the depth in the Cut may not be reduced too much near the end of the dry season. The cost of the dam will be something like six million dollars.

3. That by 1936 we must begin construction of a third set of locks to parallel the other two so we may have it ready in 1946 when needed.

4. That somewhere around 1965 we must make preparations to cut another canal in some other locality in order to have it completed when the limit of water storage on the Isthmus of Panama is reached.

7 "Security of the Panama Transit in the War"

Master Sergeant Frederick W. Hopkins, USMC
U.S. Naval Institute *Proceedings*
(March 1949): 321–26

THE PART PLAYED BY NAVAL FORCES in the security of the Panama Canal constitutes a little known but interesting fraction of the war effort during the recent period of hostilities. It is probably assumed by anyone who cares to give the matter thought that the security measures of the Navy in regard to the Canal Zone consisted of the usual Mine and Net activities, of both off-shore and in-shore sea borne patrols, and the usual close and distant aerial reconnaissance. The Army is, and was, charged with the shore defense and the security of the canal from attack and from sabotage. It is not the purpose of this essay to examine these activities, although they contributed greatly to the security of the transit. They meant to the personnel involved long and fruitless hours of standing watches, of blackout alerts, and of isolation on wild and lonely mountain tops. The dreary hours tossing on plunging decks, the tedious flights, and monotonous billets in small coastal villages and the garrison duty amounting almost to exile in the Galapagos meant to those so occupied an entirely negative participation in the war.

Appropriate measures having been taken to secure the canal from hostile sea, and/or air attack, and provision having been made by adequate guard establishments to prevent saboteurs reaching the works, it became necessary to avert the possibility of sabotage emanating from transiting ships, either from the agency of the ship itself or from personnel aboard. This duty was assigned to the Commander, Panama Sea Frontier (Commandant, Fifteenth Naval District) by the over-all Caribbean Defense Command; and it was further delegated to the District Marine Officer, who in his dual capacity as Commanding Officer of the Marine Barracks carried it out. It was necessary to co-ordinate and accomplish the wishes of the Naval and Military authorities with those of the Governor of the Panama Canal and of the Marine Superintendent by working harmoniously with the Captains of the Port at either terminus.

The methods and activities of the security forces so employed were developed through trial and error over a period of time. It is the purpose of this article to discuss the operation of the Ship Guard organization for the last eighteen months of its existence.

It was obvious that the greatest and most recurrent hazard to the transit was from ships using the waters of the area, and especially when passing through locks and narrow cuts. The possibility that a hostile crew might cause their vessel to blow up or sink in these places was great. If such an event occurred, the passage of vessels engaged in the war effort could be delayed from weeks to many months. The long and dangerous passage around South America, where submarines could lie in wait, adds over seven thousand miles to the voyage from ocean to ocean. There was also the constant danger of the fanatical individual who might blow up ship, crew, and himself, damage gates or installations by explosives, or cause a collision which, whether by accident or design, would achieve the same result.

Prevention of such an eventuality was assigned to the Naval Forces, consisting of two companies of Marines with attached naval ratings: The Second Guard Company operating from the Naval Base at Rodman (then called "Balboa, West Bank") and the Third Guard Company (located at Cristobal) from the Naval Station at Coco Solo. A Field Officer on the staff of the Commanding Officer, Marine Barracks, Balboa was designated "Co-Ordinator, Ship's Guards" and served as the general administrator of the activity. Each of the two companies consisted of from five to six officers and of about three hundred and fifty men. Twenty-five to thirty bluejackets were attached to each in the ratings of Machinist's Mate or Quartermaster. These sailors worked in pairs, one of each rating to each guard sent aboard a transiting vessel. Additional Machinist's Mates, after special instruction, served as inspectors of vessels coming to anchorage which were laden with explosives or hazardous cargoes.

Over eleven thousand vessels were passed through the canal or anchored in adjacent waters, under guard. That many flew the flags of countries under Nazi domination, or dubiously neutral, without any successful attempt against the canal proves at least in a negative way that the measures established and the organization employed were successful. It is of interest, therefore, to examine in not too great detail that system and organization.

From Limon Bay on the north or Caribbean coast of Panama, whose sheltering breakwaters provide a safe and ample anchorage, the canal traverses the Isthmus in a generally southeasterly direction. Six miles from the northern entrance and up a dredged channel are the Gatun Locks, which in three successive lifts elevate a ship to the surface of Gatun Lake, where a secondary anchorage is provided. The buoyed route of the canal is thence across the lake by a series of tangents to Gamboa, a distance of about twenty miles. Here begin the reaches of Gaillard Cut, extending through the hills and continental divide about ten miles to Pedro Miguel Locks. There a vessel is let down one lift into mile-long Miraflores Lake. After stepping down two more lifts at Miraflores Locks, about eight more miles remain through dredged channel to the Gulf of Panama. There is no terminal lake at the Pacific end, the inner anchorage being along the route of the channel and sheltered by the mole extending out to the fortified islands in the bay. The outer anchorage was in the open gulf, offshore from Taboga and Taboguilla Islands, and outside of the mine fields. The principal danger areas in the canal, where maximum damage or interruption could be effected, were obviously in the locks themselves or in the long and winding cut, especially at points opposite slide areas or where there were changes of direction. A vessel sunk at these points might effectually block the channel until removed. Undoubtedly a tremendous explosion in the Culebra reach would bring down much of the old and persistent Cucaracha slide, which has been in slow movement and under constant excavation for thirty years. Had this happened, the canal would have been closed as far as this war was concerned. The ramming of a mitre gate or a sinking or explosion in a lock chamber would have resulted in long closing of that passage. No replacement for lock gates was available nor could one have been installed if it were, as they are so huge that they must be constructed in place.

Complicating the physical problem was the administrative and legal one. By Executive Order and by Proclamation, the President of the United States had declared the Zone waters to be military areas, and broad powers were given the military high command and the Governor of the Canal Zone. Our various treaties, however, guaranteed to all nations not actually belligerent to us the right of passage. With the Baltic nations generally under Nazi control, and with others sympathetic with Germany, the flag and registry was no sure guarantee that a vessel's personnel or mission were not as hostile as that of an enemy battleship. On the other hand, vessels, property, and personnel of non-belligerent and neutral nations were entitled to all treaty rights and all of the legal rights of peacetime, as curtailed only by measures most imperative for safety. This implied the necessity of coordinating the guard activities with many agencies. Officers of the Coast Guard, under the Navy, had the jurisdiction over Maritime Laws. The Canal Zone Police enforced the local civil law. The U.S. Maritime Commission had cognizance of American personnel on U.S. registered vessels, and the Consuls of England, France, and the South American and other countries were interested in the ships and crews under their respective flags. Customs Officers of both the United States and Panama expected some cooperation from the guard in the control of smuggling. Naval Intelligence was required to investigate, clear or detain, and the Port Captains of Cristobal and Balboa directed the harbor and canal pilots and were responsible to the Marine Superintendent for the schedules and transits.

The most workable arrangement was to place each ship guard company under the operational control of the appropriate Port Captain, coordinating their activities through the officer detailed as Ship Guard Coordinator. The tactical control remained with the company commanders, thus placing upon them the responsibility for successful completion of each specific mission.

The operation developed into two separate categories; the first being aboard ships at the anchorages, where some lay for a week or more under investigation, awaiting orders, or pending transit, if classed as hazardous— that is, laden with ammunition or with inflammable liquid cargo. They were most dangerous if, after having carried high octane fuel, they had been emptied and were full of the residual, easily detonated gas-air mixture. Hazardous cargo and anchorage guards usually consisted of two Marines who were accompanied aboard by a Machinist's Mate-Inspector; the latter verified that port regulations and safety precautions were carried out or were completed by the ship's company before the vessel was cleared to the Port Captain. On numerous occasions more than thirty vessels lay under this form of security guard, either at terminal anchorages, in Gatun Lake, or at Gamboa. The necessity of this activity was frequently illustrated in the guard reports of instances of careless attempts at smoking, open lights, welding, and so forth aboard vessels carrying dangerous and even fused ammunition, explosives, or containing dangerous volatile oils or explosive gas mixtures in their holds. This duty was the most uninteresting and least inspiring, as well as the most arduous, and it met with the least cooperation on the part of the captains and crews, who occasionally resented the presence of Marines aboard. They frequently considered it an invasion of their personal rights or national sovereignty. Clashes occurred infrequently, but the Marines were well trained in their duties, inflexible in their execution of them, and fully supported by the authorities. Not over five persons were shot by Marines—none fatally—in the execution of this function, the sentry in each instance being sustained by the local board of inspectors as well as by the naval command.

Vessels to transit and time of departure from moorings, or the hours for arrival and departure of ships, were designated by the Captain of the Port affected, who notified the Guard Company assigned, and designated the forces required. The terms "Full Guard," "Modified Guard," "A" or "B" Guard, etc., were used according to a table and code to describe the various strengths and compositions. For example, a "Full Guard" consisted of an officer, a staff noncommissioned officer, and about fourteen men; a "Modified Guard" was smaller and was commanded by a senior non-commissioned officer; and so on down to a Corporal and four men. Each of the above had, in addition, two naval ratings assigned, a Machinist's Mate and a Quartermaster rate. Probably the details most frequently called out were either "Modified" or "Type A" guards. No guards were placed upon combat vessels of the United States Navy. Special "Honor" guards were placed aboard combat vessels of friendly or allied powers, these consisting of one or more officers and staff non-commissioned officers, as a courtesy, to give information and possibly to establish visibly the ultimate sovereignty of the United States in these waters. Honor Guards always wore full khaki uniform and were unarmed; occasionally khaki was prescribed for "Full Guards" when particularly appropriate, but otherwise the duty uniform of the Ship Guard Companies was utility clothing. Experience established that the nature of the work and the filthy condition of so many ships made the wearing of khaki impracticable, just as it was necessary to secure and authorize the wearing of low cut, dress shoes, the field shoe proving not only clumsy but dangerous on slippery decks and wet sea ladders. As the duration of a single one-way transit was from eight to twelve hours, men occupied in this second category of the work carried light packs containing personal articles, liberty uniform for wear at the other terminal if desired, and a lunch put up in a standard workingman's lunch box with vacuum bottle; this lunch was specially procured by the Quartermaster for this duty.

All members of the guard were forbidden to eat or drink anything from the ship's supply, this to prevent the possibility of a detail becoming poisoned or drugged while aboard. It became necessary to adopt a standard procedure for wearing the pack in small boats and while boarding. It was not generally worn while aboard, but was usually stowed at the place on deck designated by the Commander of the Guard as a rendezvous. To facilitate removal if the wearer went overboard, it was slung by the straps over one shoulder only, in an unmilitary but safe and easily discardable manner. At first the Riesing Gun was the standard arm, but the pistol and nightstick replaced them as more satisfactory, since all ship-to-shore and boarding movements were made by small boat and sea ladder.

Bearing in mind that over 11,000 vessels were handled, including those lying at anchorages, and allowing for changes of the guard and so forth, it is safe to assume that about two hundred thousand individual embarkations and disembarkations were made. Only one loss was sustained— a bluejacket who fell overboard from a launch and was apparently swept under a float by propeller wash. This infinitesimal casualty rate indicates a high degree of discipline and practice, as such movements were usually made at night or early morning, and very frequently in streaming tropical rain.

Each guard detail boarding a vessel scheduled for transit accompanied the pilot and did not leave the ship until dismissed by him, since under the law and regulations the pilot was the supreme authority while the vessel was under way in the canal. The Marine commander of the guard, upon coming aboard, officially presented to the captain of the ship a form letter authenticated by authority of the Governor, advising the master that the Zone Pilot had sole jurisdiction over navigation of the ship, and summarizing the duties and authority of the guard. All small arms were required to be turned over to the guard's keeping while in transit, and the ship's master was advised that it was the duty of the guard commander to enforce every order of the pilot and to prevent any interference with him or with his navigation of the ship. The crew was mustered and informed of the requirements and orders, to prevent any mistakes or regrettable accidents. On occasion there would be aboard one or more persons about whom Naval Intelligence had advance information, and these persons were removed or confined in a stateroom under guard in accordance with instructions received in each case. In not over half a dozen cases did a captain refuse to recognize the full authority of the pilot, and in these cases he was promptly locked up in his cabin, with no interruption to the transit. On several occasions it was necessary to confine an entire ship's company with the exception of essential engine room people, who were more heavily guarded than usual; this was possible because the Panama Canal always placed on board a crew of deck hands to handle lines and work the vessel through the locks.

Once aboard, the ship's guns would be unloaded, the breeches opened and a sentry placed over them, the anchor catted ready to let fall, and a tow cable bent to the forward bitts with a sentry placed on the forecastle—a post established to prevent any interference with the steering engines. A deck patrol was also assigned, as well as such others as might be required by the circumstances, the orders, and the character of the vessel in question. A member of the guard was always detailed to accompany the pilot to protect him and enforce his orders, and another was posted in the wheel house. Meanwhile, the naval ratings had set up a field telephone outfit they had brought aboard. The deck rating manned an instrument in the wheel house, the engine room rating being at the other end and protected by a sentry; this established independent communications from bridge to engines and precluded the possibility of any "mistakes" in transmission of orders over the ship's telegraph. Every order of the pilot in regard to speed or change of direction, or affecting the navigation, was repeated over the field phone, the naval deck rating and his Marine partner insuring that it was executed correctly by the helmsman while the engine room pair insured prompt compliance at the controls below. Orders were to shoot instantly at any apparent attempt to carry out a pilot's order in reverse, but occasion for this treatment never occurred. It is believed that crews were convinced that the Marines would do it. Compliance was so strict by engineers and helmsmen that during the period fewer than average honest errors were made, in consideration of the volume of traffic handled. Even these errors resulted in only minor mishaps and plainly were without malicious intent.

All guards were alerted and kept stations during passage through the locks and Gaillard Cut. They were permitted to secure and to relax through the reaches of Gatun Lake, unless the ship or the personnel aboard her were suspect. Upon completing a transit and being released by the pilot, the detail reported in to the company at the terminus of arrival, were fed, quartered, and permitted to go on liberty if there was sufficient time before 10:00 p.m. They were returned to their "home" company next day, either on a return guard trip, or by rail if the exchange of men did not approximately balance. The Panama Railroad carried one coach on each of the two daily round trips for this purpose. The men, often disheveled, weary, and in dirty garments, could thus travel in privacy during the two hour rail trip.

Except at peak periods, the usual practice was for a man to make two round trips a week (entailing a total of from four to five days time) although frequently they were called on for more. In consideration of this, and of the long hours entailed, the disturbed sleeping conditions, and irregular meal hours, the training periods of the Ship Guard companies were limited to schools and instruction pertaining to their specific duties. There were classes in first aid, swimming in full uniform, rescue from drowning, practice with weapons, and similar subjects. Courtesy not only in its military application but as appropriate to this particular duty was stressed. Some instruction was given in regard to ship architecture, nomenclature and practices, and in recognition of foreign flags. No training period was ever permitted to be conducted in a perfunctory manner.

The District Marine Officer supervised very closely the instruction given and was particularly insistent that no man's time be wasted. He required that men have as much free and liberty time as the conditions of the service would permit. There was in effect a local rule applying to the entire Marine garrison on the Isthmus, permitting men to apply for a change of station within the command every six months. It is notable that few if any such applications were received from members of the two companies engaged in the ship and transit operation during the period under discussion. It was pretty well understood that these requests did not have to go through official channels but could be laid on the Executive Officer's desk or slipped under his office door, so it is believed that the administration of the activity was successful in regard to the personnel involved as well as in the results obtained.

Some ingenuity and imagination was required, and much cooperation on the part of the Post Supply Officer, in operating the mess halls of these companies as "short order" houses, as it was manifestly impossible to have men present for meals at the conventional hours. Most of the accepted ritual of service messes went overboard in the effort to serve satisfying meals to small groups of men at all hours of the day and night, and in catering to the tastes and appetites of individuals whose duty hours were long, arduous, and often irritating. Subsistence upon the Navy Ration aided materially in this, as it was policy that no man was to go to bed hungry, no matter what time he was relieved; this policy resulted in many cases with four meals a day, if the box lunch was counted as a full meal.

The "re-deployment" period after the collapse of Germany was particularly difficult, and the total tonnage handled through the canal reached a tremendous relative peak. The volume of "Hazardous Cargoes" increased immeasurably as the sea borne operations became concentrated in the Pacific. This was followed almost immediately by a further post-war task upon the defeat of Japan. The anchorages and canal were almost choked with tankers arriving, departing, or awaiting orders. Laden with explosive liquids or dangerous residue gasses, unquestionably they were the most dangerous of the entire operation. It was definitely the dullest and most undesirable period to the men who were so anxiously awaiting demobilization. The more interesting transit duty had been reduced to a minimum by the Port Captains, and the Marine Superintendent cooperated to the fullest extent by removing category after category from the types of cargoes and ships requiring guards. As the year 1945 drew to a close the operation was dwindling away, and by consent of the Caribbean Defense Command it was turned over to the Provost Marshall and to the Canal Zone police authorities. This ended the participation of the Naval Forces in the war-time security measures for the protection of the Panama Canal.

A graduate of Shattuck Military School in 1918, **Master Sergeant Hopkins** enlisted in the Marine Corps in 1919. Transferring to the Marine Corps Reserve as Second Lieutenant, he saw service both afloat and ashore, including command of CCC camps. Called to active duty in 1941, he graduated from the Army Industrial College, and for three years was Camp Engineer at New River, N. C. From 1944 to 1946 he was Executive Officer and later Commanding Officer of Marines in the Canal Zone, with the temporary rank of Lieutenant Colonel. After demobilization, he re-enlisted in the Marine Corps as Master Sergeant, and is now on recruiting duty in San Francisco.

8 "The Panama Canal— An Auxiliary of the Fleet"

Captain R. S. Fahle, USN

U.S. Naval Institute *Proceedings*
(May 1954): 495–503

WITHIN THE FRAMEWORK of America's total military strength, the offensive as well as the protective potential of our seapower has, in recent years, emerged in clearer perspective than ever heretofore. The mobile offensive power of the U.S. Navy, built around fast carrier forces and logistically sustainable for indefinite periods in any area of the globe, is coming to be recognized as the most effective and quickly available military instrument of the national interest and prestige. It is an instrument whose very presence in a foreign harbor can exercise an enormous though unacknowledged restraining and stabilizing force among the inhabitants of the area.

The modern carrier has, therefore, in addition to formidable military power, a distinct and unique capability in the field of diplomacy, through which our ideology and attitudes can be projected abroad by peaceful means. Modern carrier forces may then be regarded as combining the diplomatic persuasive force of troops on the ground with the awesome authority of the ultimate weapon, having, as they now do, the capability of delivering the atomic bomb with high speed jet aircraft. Thus they are, in effect, the vehicle of widely diverse military capabilities, the bridge, so to speak, between the traditional and the ultramodern instruments of military power. As ground troops are withdrawn from tension areas throughout the world, or disengaged from front-line service (and this is certainly coming to pass) our carrier forces must be all the more ready to fill the ensuing power vacuum, so as to sustain continuity in the degree of psychological or moral pressure, the "show of force," appropriate to the local situation. It follows that the mobility of these forces on a global scale becomes increasingly vital. This mobility must be augmented by every possible means.

The number as well as the power of our modern carriers is growing apace. Six carriers of a World War II class have been modernized by the strengthening of their flight decks to accommodate high speed jet aircraft and the installation of the means for carrying and delivering the atom bomb. Three carriers of a later class, already possessing the atom bomb capability, are now scheduled for further modernization. Newly authorized carrier construction and continuing modernization of existing classes will increase the offensive potential of this force to formidable proportions and its number to more than twelve vessels. The growth and development of this immense seaborne strength is, however, accompanied by a paradoxical limitation of its capabilities. These modern carriers with their vastly extended potential suffer from a loss of mobility between the widely separated strategic areas of the Atlantic and Pacific Oceans. This situation arises from the fact that none of these vessels is able to transit the Panama Canal. Thus we are denied the fullest effectiveness in the employment of our primary seaborne weapon through the obsolescence of a vital supporting component of our seapower.

The dynamic concept which led to the construction of the Panama Canal was basically one of naval strategy. It was the implacable determination of President Theodore Roosevelt that a trans-isthmian waterway be constructed to provide the Navy with a degree of mobility between oceans, which was in that day a utopian dream. That such a waterway would at the same time become an everlasting benefit to intracoastal and worldwide shipping was of course recognized, but this idea lacked the compelling urgency of the strategic motive. The scheme was bold and revolutionary. The obstacles to be surmounted were fantastic, and the ordeals of the construction period are now recorded history. Since the official opening of the Canal in 1920, it has been the Navy's connecting link between oceans and has been so used freely and continuously by naval vessels. Through the years of unrestricted use, the Panama Canal has, however, come to be taken somewhat for granted by the Navy, so much so that for planning as well as operational purposes it is regarded in much the same light as any free and open waterway or navigable strait. This attitude has developed almost into a habit of thought until today, when we find the Canal suddenly closed (as if it had never existed) to our large carriers. The very waterway whose primary strategic purpose was to afford mobility and flexibility in the disposition of our fleet now denies those same advantages to its most potent units. A realization of this stark fact seems to call for a reassessment of the basic nature of this vital and complex installation. The closing of the Canal to our large carriers highlights the fallacy of the rather complacent and detached presumption whereby this waterway has come to be viewed as nothing more than another geographical feature. It is, in fact, a mechanism which enables oceangoing vessels to cross the Isthmus of Panama by successively raising and then lowering them a vertical distance of eighty-five feet. It is a masterpiece of engineering and precision, whose physical dimensions as well as operating capabilities are of the most vital concern to the Navy, to such an extent that our strategic planning must always be in some measure conditioned by these factors. This installation must be regarded as a vital adjunct to our seapower. Indeed, it would not appear unreasonable to recognize the Panama Canal for what it is in fact, an auxiliary of the fleet, and this to at least the same degree as any other major shore facility, shipyard, or naval base.

The blocking of the interoceanic link across the Panamanian Isthmus to our modern carriers has a profound and far-reaching effect on all naval operations and planning. Since these vessels are the core of today's naval striking forces, it avails little that the logistic support and screening elements of such a force can transit the canal, if its very nucleus can make the equivalent movement only by steaming some 8000 miles around Cape Horn. The major striking force of the Navy must therefore be so disposed that any single element of it is virtually committed at any time to one ocean or the other. The flexibility of deployment of this force, then, if not actually denied us, is at the least drastically decreased. Tactically, if not strategically, we are faced with a divided fleet—a two-ocean Navy. The most astute planning and disposition of forces, based on the most infallible intelligence, cannot cure the basic weakness inherent in this situation.

It cannot be doubted that the enemy is fully aware of this paradoxical plight, wherein our offensive seapower has, in growing, divided itself. Having had, at the outset, the classical advantage of interior lines of communication within the Eurasian land mass he now finds this asset enhanced through the further attenuation of our already far-flung exterior lines. It can be expected that this advantage will be fully exploited under circumstances of the enemy's choosing. In the sinister pattern of cold war technique, tensions can be created in any peripheral area of the Communist empire, ranging from internal strife or riots, to civil war, and finally armed intervention. In many instances such situations might be stabilized through the mere presence of a potent naval force. Armed intervention and open hostilities could in other instances be snuffed out and prevented from spreading by the swift application of naval air power in support of a vigorous diplomatic attitude. Such peripheral actions short of total war, "police actions" if you will, are a growing possibility of the future. The employment of naval air power for this purpose would preclude the need for the landing and supporting of ground troops. To be effective against quickly erupting situations in widely separated areas, however, such missions will require a high degree of mobility in the deployment of carrier forces. This flexibility of movement cannot now be achieved, owing to the loss of our own interoceanic link.

This same situation, which is a serious hindrance to our seapower under the requirements imposed by the cold war, would very likely become a disastrous road block in the crucial days following the outbreak of another world war. In the global climate of strategic power which prevails today, time, and therefore speed of movement over the earth's surface, is of the essence. The urgency of the time factor is intensified by the very ideology to which our military power is dedicated, namely, that we, as a nation, will never commit unprovoked aggression. It follows then, that our first, our very earliest, blow will be retaliatory. The application of our might is unalterably committed to the counterblow—first the parry, then the thrust, but only if the parry has succeeded, and we are indeed able to make the thrust. In such an ominous climate, it is not enough that we possess the ultimate weapons and the means of delivering them at sea, if access between the two primary strategic ocean areas, within acceptable limits of time, is to virtually withhold from the only vessels capable of accomplishing the delivery. It is evident that any world holocaust of the future would erupt with shocking suddenness, and that in this event the two critical ocean areas of the Atlantic and the Pacific would lie within the northern half of the northern hemisphere. Let it be assumed that the ensuing global situation would be such as to render the transit of the Suez Canal, if usable at all, by carrier forces, an unacceptable risk. A shift, then, of modern carrier strength from one strategic theater to the other, in order to deliver overwhelming and decisive power to a critically threatened area or to strike offensively from a point of greatest vantage, would require a voyage of approximately 8000 miles more than that of the normal trans-isthmian route. At a speed of 25 knots, disregarding the limitations of a screening force, adverse weather conditions, and added logistical requirements, this distance of itself represents a minimum time loss of 320 hours or some 13 days! It has been written that in the event of total atomic war, the crucial interval in which the issue might be decided is in the order of the first 48 hours following its outbreak. Should it happen that our Strategic Air Command sustained losses during this crucial period which would preclude the full accomplishment of its mission, the Navy's atomic capability would be needed to its fullest extent. This would be a situation of overwhelming urgency to the nation's very survival. A preventable loss of time amounting to 13 days in the transfer from one theater to the other of all, or any element, of our seaborne air power could have tragic consequences. This loss of time might well become the nail for want of which the shoe was lost.

It would seem to be clearly in the national interest, if not in fact a compelling need, that the shackles which restrain the mobility of our seapower be loosed. To acquiesce in the continued presence of the surmountable barrier which now divides our fleet is, in a sense, to betray its primary mission and to abort the sensational growth in its offensive power. And this barrier is most certainly surmountable.

As a result of deep concern over the vulnerability of the Panama Canal during the last war, the need was felt to explore in detail all possible alternate routes across the isthmus and, as a result, there was published in 1947 a comprehensive study of some 27 possible trans-isthmian canal routes. This work, known as the "Isthmian Canal Studies, 1947," was a detailed analysis of the relative feasibility of the various trans-isthmian routes extending from Tehuantepec to Darien, based on excavation and construction costs as well as operating characteristics, which were derived from actual surveys and the engineering of each route. Included in these studies was an analysis of three distinct concepts for the modernization of the present canal, each of which would combine, at the same time though in varying degree, the features of reduced vulnerability, increased lock capacity for larger vessels, and the ability to handle a greater volume of traffic.

Without attempting here to evaluate the merits of an additional canal across the Central American isthmus, it will nevertheless be of interest to examine briefly the three basic proposals for modernizing the present Panama Canal, any one of which would serve to eliminate the interoceanic roadblock to our modern carriers. Taken in order of lowest cost and greatest simplicity these are, first, the so-called "Third Locks Project," which consists merely of a third set of locks paralleling the two originally constructed at each of three locations, namely Gatun, Pedro Miguel, and

Miraflores. This third set of locks was to be located at some distance from the original installations, in order to reduce the vulnerability of the canal to bombing attacks, and the lock dimensions were to be such as to accommodate the largest foreseeable vessel. Excavation for this project was actually begun during the war as an emergency measure but was discontinued as the evolution of our two-ocean Navy, together with the withdrawal of the Japanese enemy into the western Pacific, diminished the urgency of the need. This excavation stands today in a state of partial completion. At this point it may be well to dispel the myth of vulnerability (or invulnerability) as it was conceived after World War II. The third set of locks, paralleling the original installations at three different points, would have been separated from them by a distance of something less than a mile. Since the ultimate bomb today virtually insures the complete obliteration of all installations above the ground within a radius of at least five miles of ground zero, it would appear that the item of vulnerability of the operating structures cannot be overcome in any single trans-isthmian lock canal.

The second scheme of modernization, called the "Terminal Lake Plan," incorporated this same third locks concept; however, it went further, and proposed raising the level of Miraflores Lake to that of Gatun Lake (*i.e.*, 85 feet above mean sea level), which would require raising the height of Miraflores Locks by the addition of one more chamber, thus making it the equivalent of the three chambered locks at Gatun, and eliminating entirely the single chambered locks at Pedro Miguel. The removal of the intermediate lift at Pedro Miguel and its substitution with an equivalent added lift at Miraflores would increase the depth of Miraflores Lake by some 30 feet and create a sizeable anchorage area for ocean going vessels. This would result in extending the present level of Gatun Lake and Gaillard Cut to Miraflores Locks, which then with Gatun Locks would hold all the impounded waters of the canal, while at the same time providing a terminal lake at each end of Gaillard Cut, *i.e.*, at Gatun and Miraflores. The benefits to be derived from this feature of the plan are associated with more efficient dispatching of north and southbound traffic through Gaillard Cut, the delaying of disabled vessels, and other administrative matters internal to the operation of the canal. While these benefits would no doubt lead to an increase in the efficiency of operations and the traffic capacity of the canal, they are not related to the fundamental strategic capability of transiting our largest naval vessels, which would be achieved in any case. As a consequence, this plan offers no significant advantage to the Navy which would not accrue from the Third Locks Project.

The third plan is the much discussed "Sea Level Canal." To many students of the problem this is the ideal solution to the question of a truly efficient trans-isthmian waterway. The basic engineering of this plan has been accomplished, and its results are both ingenious and dramatic. Gaillard Cut would, of course, have to be greatly deepened, and a corresponding increase in channel width is planned. All locks, in the sense that they are needed to lift a ship over land, would be eliminated. Owing to the phenomenal difference in the tidal range at the Pacific and the Atlantic sides of the isthmus, certain controlling mechanisms are required. Since the mean tidal range at the Pacific terminal is in the order of 16 feet, whereas that at the Atlantic is less than one foot, prohibitively strong currents for successful navigation of the narrow channel of Gaillard Cut would prevail at certain hours of the day. The plan therefore contemplates a set of tidal locks at Balboa, the Pacific terminal, which would be used to transit vessels during those hours when currents exceed a certain maximum for safe navigation. A free navigation channel, paralleling these tidal locks, would be open to all shipping during the hours when the tidal locks are not required. The sea level canal would thus be the nearest possible approach to an unrestricted strait between two continental land masses. While still vulnerable to the devastating effects of modern weapons, this canal would stand a vastly better chance of survival than would any other, which is dependent on impounded water needed for the lockage of vessels over a land barrier.

These three plans, together with the various alternate canal routes, have presumably been duly considered and set aside. As of today, no decision has yet been announced for the adoption of any of the modernization proposals, nor for a second trans-isthmian route. The global strategic position of our offensive seapower today demands that this whole problem be reexamined and that a decision be reached at an early date. The issue can no longer, in honesty or in logic, be postponed.

There is, moreover, a very real and practical operating feature of the Canal, which tends, of itself, to force the issue of modernization from the point of view of economical operation and maintenance. This feature is that all the heavy and intricate locks machinery requires an electrical power supply of 25 cycle alternating current. This means that the preponderance of electrical power generated in the Zone must be at this frequency, which must also serve the greater part of the community as a whole, the standard 60 cycle power being available only in limited areas. The periodic replacement then, of motor, generator, or control components in order to keep the present locks in operation, requires procurement of such items in the U.S. at exorbitant cost on a custom basis, since the electrical industry in this country no longer produces standard equipment designed for 25 cycles. The time must come, if it has not already, when such uneconomical maintenance can no longer be justified. The need for an early decision with respect to the modernization of the Panama Canal is thus further reinforced.

The Navy, apart from its basic and most vital interest in the Panama Canal, has actually had a degree of control over its day-to-day operations which is not generally known. Since the historic task of constructing the canal was completed under the direction of the U.S. Army Engineer Corps, it was not too illogical that the operation of the canal and the administration of the Canal Zone Government be continued under the Department of the Army, with a general officer of the Army Engineer Corps as Governor. Thus was the organization originally set up. In recognition, however, of the Navy's vital interest in the waterway as a whole, there was established a Marine Division to control the transit operations through the canal and a Mechanical Division to operate the drydocks and extensive ship repair facilities, both of these organizations being headed by a qualified U.S. Navy captain who reported directly to the Governor.

The Marine Division under the direction of the Marine Superintendent controls canal operations through two Port Captains, also captains in the U.S. Navy, at the terminal ports of Balboa and Cristobal. These two officers, assisted by a competent civilian staff of pilots, tugboat operators, admeasurers, dispatchers, and clerical personnel, exercise control over all harbor movements, and schedule all north and southbound traffic through the canal, thus in effect also directing the operations of the locks. Clearance is granted to vessels by the Port Captain at the terminal port of departure when it has been determined that the payment of transit tolls and other accrued charges has been made, and that the vessel is ready for sea. Transit tolls are based on the actual volumetric measurement of each vessel, as originally made, or subsequently verified by Panama Canal admeasurers before each transit, such measurement being made under an elaborate set of internationally accepted rules. In the event of an accident in the canal, which results in damage to a vessel, the Port Captain having jurisdiction is required to conduct an investigation to establish liability for the damage, as between the Panama Canal and the vessel's owners or underwriters. The entire operation is broad in scope and complex in detail. It requires daily contact by the Port Captains with pilots, masters, steamship agents, consular officials, and others, in a variety of diverse situations. An additional function of the Marine Division is the maintenance and upkeep of all visual navigation aids, including not only the many lights and buoys in the canal and its approach channels, but also the outlying lights along both coasts of the isthmus, extending from the lighthouse on Jicarita Island in the Gulf of Panama, to Isla Grande Lighthouse in the Gulf of Darien. It is of interest to note that the jurisdiction of the Marine Division alone, in the matter of vessel clearances, investigation of marine accidents, and maintenance of light houses, is that of the Coast Guard in the continental United States.

The Mechanical Division, on the other hand, operates an extensive installation of shops and ship repair facilities, including a drydock at each terminal port, which is nearly comparable in scale to a continental naval shipyard. This division under the direction of an E.D. captain, assisted by one other E.D. naval officer, performs all major and minor ship repairs required locally by naval or commercial vessels, as well as Panama Canal tugs, dredges, and other craft. Its strategic importance, particularly that of the 1000-foot drydock at Balboa, is highlighted by the fact that the nearest comparable naval facility is situated at Norfolk on the East Coast and Terminal Island on the West Coast, some 1800 and 2900 miles distant, respectively.

The Navy, thus, indirectly exercises a significant degree of control over the operations of the Panama Canal through the five naval officers assigned to key positions on the staff of the Governor, although no direct chain of authority exists between them and the Navy Department, nor does the Commandant, 15th Naval District have authority to intervene in any question pertaining to the administration of the Panama Canal.

As of June, 1951, the organization which operated the Panama Canal and administered the Canal Zone Government had developed, since the construction days, into an administrative anachronism. While the canal continued through the years to function most efficiently, there grew, like a plant in the humid tropical environment, a sprawling bureaucracy of pseudo-autonomous bureaus and divisions staffed with civil service employees, each reporting directly to the Governor. Superimposed on this organizational anomaly was a complex and highly compartmented system of fiscal accountability, operating on an annual Congressional appropriation, at the same time that all canal tolls and revenues were annually deposited in the U.S. Treasury. As operating costs through the years increased, while revenues accruing from toll rates established in 1938 remained almost static, a growing annual deficit began to appear. This situation led to a Presidential Proclamation in March of 1948 announcing an increase in the basic transit toll rate from $.90 to $1.00 per measurement ton. Such was the outcry from intracoastal shipping interests at this proclamation, however, that its effective date was four times postponed by subsequent proclamations, over a period of two and one half years, to await the recommendations of certain Congressional committees, whose representatives made repeated visits to the Canal Zone in an effort to resolve the matter. To audit such bewildering accounts in order to determine the advisability of increased tolls and tariffs proved, however, to be virtually impossible, and several Congressional groups, of solemn purpose and high resolve, became hopelessly bogged in this sticky morass.

Meanwhile, in an effort to reduce operating costs, drastic reductions in force and curtailment of activities throughout the entire organization were instituted. Hardest hit in the course of this retrenchment was the Mechanical Division, which had been waging a valiant struggle to finance its rising plant maintenance and overhead costs in the face of a steadily diminishing work load. Operating as it was, in its own sphere of fiscal accountability, the Mechanical Division was ultimately forced, with the Governor's approval, to close the Balboa shops and the huge No. 1 drydock. Some several hundred skilled employees in the crafts category were discharged as a consequence and are no longer available in the Canal Zone. These facilities could, of course, be reactivated, but only at great cost, and subject to the time delay incident to inducing qualified skilled craftsmen to accept employment and establish residence in the Canal Zone. The Marine Division, while earning the preponderant percentage of the total canal revenues, was paradoxically not subject to the same arbitrary system of accountability and as a consequence was not hurt by the purge.

The Presidential Proclamation of March 26, 1948, establishing an increase in the transit toll rates, was finally, after four postponements of its effective date, revoked entirely by a Presidential Proclamation issued on September 29, 1950. At the same time the Act of September 26, 1950, Public Law 841, was approved by the President. This statute authorized a complete reorganization of the financial and administrative structure of the Panama Canal. Under its provisions, those units responsible for operating the canal proper and all its maintenance and repair facilities, together with the organization formerly known as the Panama Railroad Company, with its fleet of three large passenger vessels, are now incorporated as the Panama Canal Company. Those units engaged in certain community services as well as the functions of health, sanitation, schools, and matters of civil government, are now consolidated as the Canal Zone Government. Both of these major organizations operate under the direction of the Governor of the Canal Zone.

The Panama Canal Company is a government-owned corporation, which is to be self-supporting. It is intended that the cost of operating the canal, as well as approximately fifty per cent of the cost of administering the Canal Zone Government, will be met by the revenues earned by the corporation. The remaining cost of administering the government will be met by revenues accruing from such collateral business activities as hotels, commissaries, and clubhouses. In addition to meeting the above costs of operation and administration, the corporation is required to pay annually into the U.S. Treasury an amount sufficient to cover the annual annuity payment to the Republic of Panama required under the treaty of 1936, the interest on the original capital investment in the canal installations, as well as compensation for the salaries of officers of the Army, Navy, and Public Health Service attached to the corporation or the Canal Zone Government. As an offset against this requirement, military and other government vessels will no longer be entitled to toll free transit but will be charged transit tolls, which will not be paid in cash but will be entered as a credit on the books of the corporation. With the financial structure thus established, the Act further authorizes the Panama Canal Company, subject to the approval of the President, to prescribe and to change the transit toll rates from time to time as necessary to meet operating costs of the canal and to change the rules for the measurement of vessels.

It can be expected that under this new organization a state of solvency will eventually be achieved, and that the efficiency of management will in time approach that of any other business corporation. The reorganization has been accompanied by a drastic streamlining throughout and a considerable consolidation of divisions and bureaus. This is of interest to the Navy only to the extent that the naval or maritime functions of the canal are affected, and in this respect there has resulted a consolidation of the Marine Division and the Mechanical Division into a Marine Bureau of the Panama Canal Company, headed by the Marine Director. The former Mechanical Division, its internal organization still intact, is now the Industrial Division of the Marine Bureau. All transit, operating, and maintenance functions of the canal proper are thus vested in the Marine Bureau, which is composed of six subordinate units. These are: the offices of the Port Captains at Balboa and Cristobal, the Locks Division, the Dredging Division, the newly designated Industrial Division, and the Aids to Navigation Section. The five naval officers occupying the key positions in this key bureau of the Panama Canal Company are the Marine Director, the two Port Captains, the Chief of the Industrial Division (E.D.), and his assistant.

Whatever the organizational structure of this corporation, and regardless of its position in the executive branch of the Federal government, it is evident that the Navy's interest in this strategic installation, this supporting component of the fleet, must transcend any other incidental consideration. Hand in hand with this overriding interest there must exist a corresponding degree of responsibility for (or at least participation in) policy decisions affecting its capabilities and operating characteristics. This being so, the question of initiative in such matters arises. Who, for example, should take the initiative in making recommendations with respect to the question of modernizing the Panama Canal, or reactivating its major ship repair facilities? Can matters of such scope and strategic significance properly be delegated to the Marine Director of the Panama Canal Company, a Navy captain whose views or recommendations, if any, would have to pass through the Governor of the Canal Zone before being considered at departmental level? Has not the time come when the Navy must take the initiative and press vigorously for action which will make the Panama Canal able once more to serve all of the fleet?

Graduated from the U.S. Naval Academy in the Class of 1931, **Captain Fahle** was the Executive Officer of USS *Ludlow* during the North African invasion and was Commanding Officer of USS *Downes* during the Marianas and Philippine Campaigns in 1944. In 1950–51 he served as Assistant to the Marine Director at Balboa, Canal Zone, and later as Captain of the Port, Cristobal, Canal Zone. At present he is the District Intelligence Officer, Headquarters, 13th Naval District.

"Prognosis for the Panama Canal"

9

August C. Miller Jr.

U.S. Naval Institute *Proceedings*
(March 1964): 64–73

That magnificent portion [of America], situated between the two oceans, will in time become the emporium of the universe. Its canals will shorten the distances of the world, and will strengthen the commercial ties of Europe, America and Asia.—Simon Bolivar, 1815.

THE PANAMA CANAL, now approaching its sixtieth year, still ranks as one of the world's foremost engineering feats. Ten years in the making, the Canal was formally opened five months ahead of schedule when the Pacific Railway's SS *Ancon* made the first official ocean-to-ocean transit on 15 August 1914. Essentially, the same locks, gates, and machinery are still in use, but the Canal is reaching the limit of its capacity and is too narrow for the new large tankers, the great ore ships, and the super aircraft carriers.

Furthermore, the Canal is facing the threatening cross-current of Panamanian nationalism. The United States must soon make both technical and political decisions on issues which have been simmering for half a century. In the light of changing times, it is necessary for us to take a new look at our relationship to Panama and the Canal.

The United States had long been interested in a canal through Central America. As early as 1825, Secretary of State Henry Clay, in a message to an inter-American conference sponsored by Simon Bolivar, urged consideration of an isthmian canal whose benefits would be available to all nations. The California gold rush crossings across the Isthmus of Panama, in 1849, emphasized the need for a ship passage. Toward the end of the century, the requirement for a waterway across the Isthmus was dramatized by the fact that the battleship *Oregon* took three months under forced draught to travel 13,400 miles from the Pacific Ocean to Cuban waters by way of the Straits of Magellan.

A French company, the Compagnie Universelle, under the leadership of Ferdinand de Lesseps, builder of the Suez Canal, obtained a concession from Colombia and made the first attempt, in 1881, to dig a canal across the Isthmus of Panama. But the company went bankrupt before two-fifths of the work was done. A new corporation (Compagnie Nouvelle) was organized to take over and salvage what it could.

When the dynamic Theodore Roosevelt became President of the United States, he was determined to promote the completion of the canal. For T. R., greatly influenced by Captain A. T. Mahan, the building of the canal was an integral part of the development of U.S. sea power. The U.S. Congress made provision for a canal through the Isthmus of Panama with the passage of the Spooner Bill of 29 June 1902. Philippe Bunau-Varilla, agent for Compagnie Nouvelle, agreed to sell all the French rights and canal-building equipment to the United States for 40 million dollars. The Hay-Harran treaty was drawn up, by which Colombia, the nation which then included what is now the Republic of Panama, was to receive a 10-million-dollar payment and an annual rental of $250,000 for leasing a 6-mile-wide canal zone to the United States. The treaty also authorized the French company to sell its property to the United States. Colombia by this agreement was to retain its sovereignty over the zone. The Colombian Senate early in 1903 failed to ratify this treaty.

On 2 November 1903, the day before a revolution broke out, which was bloodless except for the deaths of one bystander and a donkey, the American gunboat USS *Nashville* appeared in Panama harbor. By the terms of the Bidlack-Mallarino Treaty of 1846 with Colombia, the United States had the right to intervene in the event of disorder and maintain an open transit route on the Isthmus to Panama City to suppress the center of revolt. Acting on this basis, the American-owned trans-isthmian railway paradoxically refused to transport Colombian troops across the Isthmus to Panama City to suppress the center of revolt. On 4 November, the revolutionary junta declared Panama independent, and two days after that the United States recognized *de facto* the new Republic of Panama, and made immediate plans for a canal treaty.

The Hay-Bunau-Varilla Treaty, signed in 1903 between the United States and the newly born Republic of Panama, permitted us to construct the Canal. By that treaty, as stated in Article II, Panama granted to the United States "in perpetuity," the "use, occupation and control" of the land and water areas now included within the 533 square miles of the Canal Zone. Article III of the treaty specifically granted to the United States "all the rights, power, and authority within the Zone . . . which the United States would possess and exercise if it were the sovereign of the territory . . . to the entire exclusion of the exercise by the Republic of Panama of any such sovereign rights, power or authority."

The United States agreed to pay Panama 10 million dollars in gold and $250,000 annually, and guaranteed Panama's independence. Panama has felt that her hastily signed treaty was much less favorable than the one negotiated by the United States with Colombia, which the Colombian Parliament refused to ratify. This, then, is the basis of nationalist demands for sovereignty in the Canal Zone.

The wording of the treaty, "if it were the sovereign," implied that Panama retained title to the Zone, even though it renounced its right to exercise its sovereignty there. This concept of "titular sovereignty" is equated by some Panamanians with the full substance of sovereignty, and they claim simply that "the canal is ours."

A group of very able Panamanian lawyers places a limited interpretation on the 1903 treaty. They contend that the 1903 grant is only for the purpose of building, maintaining, and defending a canal, and that powers not specifically delegated are reserved to Panama—a subtle implication that the Canal Zone belongs to Panama. Early in the Suez crisis of August 1956, Secretary of State John Foster Dulles made the statement in a press conference that "the United States did not fear nationalization of the Panama Canal," because it had "the rights of sovereignty" there. Foreign Minister Aquilino Boyd of the Republic of Panama countered with a forceful restatement of Panama's historical position: "There is no doubt that the treaty of 1903 does not grant the United States sovereignty over the Canal Zone." Panama's claims in 1961 to legal jurisdiction over the waters extending 12 miles beyond its shores, and thus control of the maritime entrances to the Canal, further emphasize its desire to extend some effective control over Canal operations.

The Hay-Bunau-Varilla Treaty has been twice amended, but no changes were made to the key Articles II and III which define sovereignty. A 1936 treaty rescinded the U.S. guaranty of Panama's political independence and the concomitant right of intervention in Panama. But the United States still retained the right to defend the Canal in the event of war. Payments for the use of the Canal were raised to $430,000. A 1955 treaty increased annuity payments to 1.93 million dollars. But the Republic's request for the replacement of the "perpetuity" clause in the Zone grant by a 99-year renewable lease was rejected.

It is this issue of sovereignty which has helped to bring about deteriorating relations between the United States and the Republic of Panama. In November 1959, two attempts were made by Panamanian mobs to plant the flag of Panama in the Canal Zone as a symbol of sovereignty. On 17 September 1960, President Dwight D. Eisenhower declared that the flag of Panama would be displayed jointly with the flag of the United States in Shaler's Triangle, a public plaza in the Canal Zone, as "visual evidence" of Panama's titular sovereignty. The President's order was issued over the objections of many Pentagon leaders, Congressional officials, and the Army. It should be noted that the United States has always recognized the titular sovereignty Panama over the Canal Zone, and Deputy Under Secretary of State Livingston Merchant on a visit to Panama in 1959 made a very clear restatement of this principle. On 10 January 1963, President John F. Kennedy extended this concession by announcing that the flag of the Republic of Panama would be flown together with the flag of the United States of America on land in the Canal Zone where the flag of the United States of America is flown by civilian authorities.

The Panama Canal is approximately 50 miles long—from deep water to deep water—and the Canal Zone, which slices right through the heart of Panama, is ten miles wide. Some 53,000 people live in this Zone, with U.S. citizens comprising approximately seven-tenths of the population. About 39,000 persons in the Canal Zone are civilians; the rest are military personnel attached to U.S. armed forces stationed in the Zone.

The United States purchased land rights to the Canal Zone for 40 million dollars, from the French Compagnie Nouvelle, but this was only the first installment of the huge cost of building and operating the Canal. When it was completed, in 1914, the cost had reached 380 million dollars. To date, the U.S. government has invested 1.7 billion dollars in this enterprise. About 1 billion dollars of this amount has been returned in toll fees and other income. Since the Canal opened in August 1914, more than 1.2 billion long tons of cargo have been carried through it by more than 300,000 vessels of all types.

The Canal itself is owned by the United States and operated by the Panama Canal Company, a government corporation set up by Congress in 1950. It operates as a self-supporting corporate enterprise and meets not only its own operating expenses, but also pays the costs of the Canal Zone government, interest, and depreciation charges on the U.S. investment in the Canal, and $430,000 of the Republic of Panama's annuity.

In the Zone, the Panama Canal Company runs or regulates all business enterprises including the commissaries, restaurants, and recreational activities, assigns living quarters to the inhabitants, and in general runs what can be described as a benevolent state socialism. The Company employs 14,500 persons, 11,000 of whom are Panamanians.

The Canal Zone Government administers the civil government of the Zone and operates the police and fire departments, health and sanitation facilities, and the schools. The governor of the Zone, appointed by the President of the United States, and the President of the Canal Company are the same person—a major general of the Corps of Engineers. The Zone is also headquarters for the Commander in Chief, U.S. Southern Command.

The country of Panama is 480 miles long from east to west and varies in width from 30 to 120 miles. Its population, in 1959, was estimated at 1,029,000. Panama has been described as being more a geographical area than a viable country. Panama's economic dependence on the Canal is great. The Canal is to Panama what oil is to Saudi Arabia, copper to Chile, and tin to Bolivia—a great natural resource. In 1961, Canal Zone employees and various U.S. agencies spent well over 70 million dollars in Panama, seven million dollars more than Panama's national budget.

Over the years, the United States has poured hundreds of millions of dollars into Panama. The Canal has also brought trade and tourists to Panama. As a result of the benefits of the Canal, the United States being the chief importer of Panama's products, and borrowing investments of private American capital, Panama has one of the highest annual per capita incomes ($415.00) in Latin America. But the Canal has had the adverse effect of creating a badly balanced economy. Instead of developing its economy, Panama has been content to live off the Canal.

Unfortunately, this income is unequally distributed. Wealth and power are concentrated in the hands of a few. A third of the Panamanian populace is crowded into the urban areas of Panama City, Colón, and David, with many of the people living in slums. In Panama City, the wage scale is 35 to 40 cents an hour—just about half the amount which is paid Panamanians doing similar work in the Canal Zone. Unemployment, affecting approximately 12 per cent of the country's labor force, is concentrated in the cities. The other two-thirds of the population are scattered throughout the rugged rural area and exist as poor farmers. According to observers on the scene, various viewpoints on the U.S. occupation of the Zone prevail in Panama. In general, the Panamanians want more and better jobs in the Zone, more wages, better housing, better food, and a bigger share of so-called profits from the Canal for Panama. Some have complained about the alleged failure of Zone residents to mix with Panamanians. But this has been modified considerably by "Operation Friendship," sponsored by the military commander of the U.S. Southern Command to encourage friendly contacts between military personnel in the Zone and their Panamanian neighbors.

It can be said that the country represents in microcosm most of the difficulties of Latin-American countries: illiteracy, ignorance, poverty, political and economic inequality, and social injustice. First and foremost, far too few—a rich oligarchy of 30 to 50 old families, mainly of Spanish blood—have far too much of the material wealth at the expense of the Negroes, Indians, and Mestizos who comprise 85 per cent of Panama's population. The oligarchs dominate the social, political, and economic life of the country, and the presence of the United States in the Canal Zone provides a convenient "scapegoat" for the oligarchy's misrule of Panama. In the past, the oligarchs have been able to direct the massed Panamanian resentment against them into nationalist opposition against the United States.

The changes Panama needs are in answer to problems that are agitating many Latin-American countries. They may be listed as follows: social and land reforms, an efficient tax system, low-cost housing, and a "supervisory" class of skilled administrators, teachers, and tradesmen. Another great problem is Panama's population explosion; in ten years the population has increased by 32 per cent. Since the economy's growth rate cannot keep pace with the birth rate, social discontent will continue to be widespread.

The Alliance for Progress has come on the scene as our country's first big effort to improve the economic and social conditions in Panama. The years 1961 and 1962 saw direct grants in millions of dollars, enlarged technical assistance under the Point-4 Program, and substantial loans from the Inter-American Development Bank. Full co-operation of Panamanians and particularly of the "governing elite" is needed to make this program a success. The United States alone cannot raise the standard of social, economic, and political performance in Panama. Continued announcements of Panama's participation in the program and her plans to widen the country's economic base are indeed encouraging.

It is no overstatement to indicate that there are many Panamanians who are envious of U.S. citizens in the Canal Zone. To the poor and unemployed of Panama, the Canal has always stood out as a shining island of prosperity in their midst. To them, the Zone appears to be a veritable paradise because everyone has a job, there is good housing at fair rentals, dependable utilities at fair prices; free education of high quality, and government stores with fair prices. The chief complaint of the Panamanians comes from the feeling that their extra-territorial concessions to the United States impair Panamanian sovereignty and are without adequate compensation.

There never has been a time in the 50-year history of the Canal as a going concern when relations between Panama and the United States have not been to some extent troubled, and at times bitter. At the time that the 1955 Treaty with Panama was ratified, with its earlier stated financial adjustments, many of these troubles were believed eliminated. It was a generous treaty, in that it bettered the Panamanian economy by restricting the use of commissaries and post exchanges to residents, of the Zone, transferred title to millions of dollars' worth of buildings and property outside the Zone to Panama, and provided equal base pay in any equal job for U.S. and Panamanian workers. The treaty also committed the United States to buy all its commissary supplies either in the United States or in Panama "unless not feasible to do so."

Many U.S. residents of the Canal Zone criticized the treaty as making excessive concessions to Panama at the expense of the U.S. Treasury and U.S. citizens employed in the Zone. But extreme nationalism in Panama since 1955, at times encouraged by small but vocal Communist groups and left-wing student unions, has made new and intensified demands on the United States. In November 1959, when anti-American riots took place and an attempted invasion of the Canal Zone by Panamanian Nationalists occurred, relations between the two countries became strained and seemingly irreconcilable.

After Panamanian President Roberto F. Chiari came to Washington in June 1962, bringing Panama's complaints to President Kennedy, the two presidents named a four-man commission to discuss the points of dissatisfaction and to iron out the difficulties between the two nations within the framework of existing treaties.

These special presidential representatives of the United States and Panama concluded their year-long talks on 23 July 1963. In a joint communique they announced agreement on the creation of a binational Labor Advisory Committee which will consider labor disputes arising between Panamanian employees and Canal Zone authorities. The United States has agreed to withhold and remit to Panama income taxes for which Panamanian Zone employees are liable. On other labor matters both sides discussed equal employment opportunities for Panamanians employed in the Zone, and the United States has agreed to ask Congress to make available to Panamanian employees in the Canal Zone the same health and life insurance benefits which are available to U.S. employees.

The U.S. representatives also indicated that the United States is preparing proposals for Panama's consideration to meet requests by Panama that it be given jurisdiction over a corridor through the Canal Zone connecting the capital city with the rest of the territory and that two piers in Cristobal be licensed to the Colón free zone. Other pending issues are now to be resolved through normal diplomatic channels.

Panamanian governmental officials would like to have seen this commission become a negotiating body for a new treaty with enormous economic advantages for Panama. But the United States is unlikely to agree to a new treaty until a decision has been reached concerning the construction of a new sea-level canal in Panama by nuclear excavation. Such a decision may not be forthcoming for several years yet, but in the meantime Panama will continue to press for further concessions. It is no secret that the Panamanians want a substantial increase in tolls. They argue that the rates of 90 cents a ton for laden merchant ships, 72 cents a ton for ships in ballast, and 50 cents a ton for warships and other craft are not in line with modern shipping costs. The cry is for a raise in tolls with 20 per cent of total revenues going to Panama.

Five per cent of the world's shipping goes through the Panama Canal. Approximately 15 per cent of that is intercoastal trade. The Panama Canal is of great importance to trade between Asia, Australia, and Europe and of tremendous value to the United States and Latin America—especially to the west coast nations of Ecuador, Chile, and Peru. Eighty-five per cent of the shipping tonnage of the west coast South American countries goes through the Canal.

The world's shipping in the Canal continues to increase in volume year after year. Millions of tons of oil are carried by tankers from coast to coast and strategic raw materials—copper, manganese, tin, lead, zinc—essential to the U.S. economy in peace and war, pass through the Canal. The average cargo ship by her eight-hour transit through the Canal saves 20 days of steaming and $50,000 on the voyage between San Francisco and New York.

The fiscal year 1962 set a Canal record for putting through commercial ships that ply the high seas. Some 11,150 vessels made the transit from ocean to ocean. Vessels flying the flags of the United States, Norway, Britain, West Germany, Liberia, and Japan, in that order, accounted for just about two-thirds of the transits. These ore ships, tankers, and fruit ships that ply Gatun Lake are the lifeblood of trade, and, incidentally, this year was the first in which commercial vessels of more than 300 net tons topped the 11,000 mark. It was the third straight year when such traffic exceeded 10,000 in number. Gross intake of tolls and toll credits for 1962 amounted to 58.4 million dollars—a figure approximately six per cent above the 1961 total. A marked increase in the size of the ships is evident when one observes that in 1951, ten ships of over 18,000 registered tons transited the waterway; in 1961, ships of this size numbered 330.

Military analysts have downgraded the strategic importance of the Canal, since in a worldwide nuclear war, the Canal could not be defended. But the Canal is of great importance to the security of the United States in limited wars such as those of Korea or Lebanon. In any period of diplomatic crisis involving the shifting of Pacific and Atlantic Fleets, the Canal is of great value. This was impressively demonstrated during the Cuban crisis of 1962 when we had to move quickly key amphibious units from California to Cuban waters. The Associated Press reported that on 6 November 1962 commercial traffic had to be curtailed while 17 Atlantic-bound U.S. warships passed through the Canal. Admiral J. S. Russell, U.S. Navy, testifying before a Foreign Affairs Committee in 1960 on the military value of the Canal, declared that the greatest current threat to commerce on the sea in time of war

is the submarine fleet of Soviet Russia, which today has a peace-time strength about equal to Hitler's maximum number of operational submarines at the height of World War II. To reinforce the Pacific antisubmarine forces off the California coast with a squadron of destroyers from the vicinity of the Virginia Capes would entail 21 days' steaming [via the Straits of Magellan] versus eight days via the canal.

In any limited war the "Big Ditch" would pay its way by savings in both time and money. It is true that the Forrestal-class aircraft carrier, with a 129-foot beam, cannot squeeze through the 110-foot width of the Canal's locks. But the polaris-firing nuclear-powered submarines, the new missile cruisers, modern frigates, and new antisubmarine warfare vessels, which are fast becoming the most important ships in our Navy, are small enough to pass through the Canal's present locks. During World War II, some 5,300 combat vessels and 8,300 military auxiliaries transited the Canal, while hundreds of troopships and Navy vessels passed through the Canal in the Korean engagement. Hanson Baldwin, astute military analyst, has said that Defense Department officials contend "that in a strategic sense, using the term as inclusive of political, economic and military factors, the Panama Canal is more important today than it has ever been and that, in the future, its purely military importance may increase."

During World War II, the United States spent 75 million dollars digging a third set of locks to handle bigger ships and provide another passage if the other sets were destroyed. Work was stopped on this venture in 1942 when it appeared that men and material were more critically needed elsewhere. The locks are now considered too vulnerable and too expensive to complete.

A number of short-term improvements are now being made in the Canal which will make it possible by 1980 for 60 ships a day, rather than 30, to make the crossing of the Canal. The eight-mile stretch called the Gaillard Cut, which is the present Canal's bottleneck, is being widened from 300 feet to 500 feet and deepened by five feet in order to permit two-way traffic for the larger vessels. This job is more than half done, and the final cost is expected to be around 60 million dollars. Also, the United States is preparing to build a two-mile-long lake, besides the present Gatun and Madden Lakes, to ensure an adequate water supply for canal operation when the Canal's maximum capacity is reached 1980.

Other improvements in progress include the purchase of new and more powerful towing locomotives, the installation of a lighting system along the Canal banks through the Gaillard Cut, and the installation of an electronic ship-dispatching and marine control system to permit maximum use of the locks. But all of these changes are merely makeshift, for the Canal's days are definitely numbered, and a new canal will be imperative.

As of 1 May 1963, big merchant ships are now able to handle cargo earning thousands of dollars more freight on each transit of the Panama Canal because half a foot—from 36.5 to 37 feet—has been added to the permissible draft of vessels using the waterway. The six-inch increase in permissible draft means a rise in cargo-carrying capacity of from 150 to 180 tons an inch for the large ships affected. This increase adds nothing to the tolls a ship pays for its passage through the Canal. The maximum size of merchant ships currently transiting the Canal is 102-foot beam, 800-foot length, by 37-foot draft. On 15 July 1963, the *Nagano*, a Liberian-registered ship carried the heaviest cargo ever moved in the waterway. This ship, which is 757 feet long and 102 feet wide, was laden with 48,218 long tons of iron ore bound from Guayacan, Chile, for Sparrows Point, Maryland.

Ever since the 1956 Suez Canal crisis, there has been some advocacy for internationalizing the Panama Canal. Various proposals have been recommended from time to time which would place the Canal under the control of (1) the United Nations or (2) the Organization of American States. Professors Martin B. Travis and James T. Watkins, foreign affairs specialists, have stated the case for internationalization by writing in *Foreign Affairs,* April 1959, that "internationalization would leave unimpaired the real interests of the United States, namely, the preservation of the Canal and access to it, good service at low cost, and a voice in the operation of the Canal. The security of the Canal would be, if anything, enhanced." Those who object to internationalization under UN supervision believe sabotage could be more easily committed and that policing would be more difficult. A Northwestern University study prepared in 1959 for the Senate Foreign Relations Committee proposed regionalizing the Canal under the aegis of the OAS as a means of avoiding the political dilemma of internationalizing it through a divided UN.

Before the 1956 London Conference on Suez, the Western Powers considered proposing to Nasser that he internationalize the Suez Canal. A proposal was made by some political leaders in the United States that

the Panama Canal should be internationalized first, and this would provide Nasser a face-saving precedent for doing the same with the Suez
Canal. It was also recalled at this time, that in 1945 at the Potsdam conference, President Truman in an "off-the-cuff" remark had urged the internationalizing of all the major inland waterways of the world, including
the Suez, Panama, and Kiel Canals.

But U.S. international lawyers were quick to point out that the two
canals were legally and politically far apart. The Suez Canal was run by
the Suez Canal Company, an international organization with a 99-year
lease (to expire in 1968) from Egypt, which retained sovereignty over
the Canal. The 1888 Treaty of Constantinople guaranteed the freedom
of the Suez Canal "in time of war as in time of peace, to every vessel of
commerce or of war without distinction of flag."

In contrast to this international character of the Suez Canal, the Panama Canal was operated by the U.S. government in a zone over which
it received from Panama perpetual rights equivalent to sovereignty in
the Treaty of 1903. There was no international convention giving other
countries any rights at all in the Panama Canal, except for a treaty with
the United Kingdom (Hay-Pauncefote of 1901) which established rules
for free and open navigation for vessels of commerce and war, and guaranteed the United Kingdom the right to have the same tolls for its vessels
as are charged for ours.

When Panama failed to get a bid to the Suez Conference at London,
Panamanian officials and the press protested. They claimed that Panama
was most certainly entitled to an invitation, since the world's ninth-largest
merchant fleet was flying Panama's flag and was a heavy user of the Suez.
The British Foreign Office received a note from Panama at this time,
emphasizing that the Panama Canal was on Panamanian territory "with
Panama the titular sovereign of the Canal Zone despite having granted
certain rights to the United States for specific purposes relative to maintenance, sanitation, operation and protection of the canal. . . ."

In a welcoming address to Latin American legal experts meeting in Panama City for a discussion of international waterways in 1957, Foreign Minister Aquilino Boyd of Panama cited the similarities between the Suez and Panama Canals and was quoted as saying that "in both cases Egypt and Panama reserved territorial sovereignty for themselves and granted only the concession for international public service."

Should the United States decide to leave the Zone, the Zone and the Canal would revert, of course, to full Panamanian sovereignty. But few Panamanians really want international control of the Canal in any form. Numerous official statements have been made on this subject. On 20 August 1956, the Panamanian Minister to Egypt, Rafael Vallerino, said that his government would never accept international control over the Panama Canal. President Ernesto de la Guardia, Jr., declared on 22 May 1959: "There is a time for everything but this is not the time for tampering with the present arrangement on the canal. It is simpler for us to deal with one nation over canal affairs than to deal with twenty. I believe in the sense of justice of the United States. We might be slow in our deliberations but we will eventually get together."

Informed Panamanians, however, realize that Panama would benefit less from internationalization than from the existing arrangement. Furthermore, relationships with an international authority could be more difficult. Placing the Canal in the hands of the UN could involve the obstructive tactics of the Communist bloc and misuse of the veto power. With the present political instability existing in a number of Latin-American countries, a real doubt exists as to how effective OAS control of the Canal could be. Nor do Panamanians want to run the Canal, for they well recognize the complexities of the lock system and the skills needed to operate the Canal, which only U.S. citizens now possess. It is doubtful if anyone could run the Canal more profitably than the Panama Canal Company and the Defense Department. Interrupted operation would mean the loss of canal revenues and Panama's 70-million dollar-a-year income, which is nearly one fourth of her gross national product.

To put it bluntly, what Panama really desires is for the United States to continue its Present functions, on a revised treaty basis, acknowledging Panama's sovereignty and paying more for the privilege.

The U.S. Congress is now studying a bill that would authorize a complete review of the problems and possibilities of a second Panama Canal. The need for another canal arises from the fact that shipping traffic is growing so fast in the original Panama Canal that sometime between 1980 and 2000 the "Big Ditch" will be glutted with ships, if the present traffic growth pattern continues.

When President Chiari of Panama was in Washington, in June 1962, he and President Kennedy discussed briefly the possibility of a new canal. It is interesting to note that the communiqué issued after their talks did not refer to a new treaty which Panamanian nationalists asserted should be negotiated, nor was the "sovereignty" issue mentioned. The fact that another canal may be built, perhaps in another country takes some of the steam out of the "sovereignty" issue for Panamanian nationalists.

Over the past 20 years as many as 16 routes for another canal have been considered, including one in Nicaragua, one across Tehuantepec Isthmus in Mexico, another in Costa Rica, and several in Panama.

The three routes under major consideration currently are as follows:

- The second site in Panama is called the Caledonian route and would extend for 62 males from Caledonia Bay (Atlantic side) to the Gulf of San Miguel, connecting by means of the Sabana River.
- In Panama, the San Blas route—one of two sites selected between the present Canal and the Colombian border would start in the Gulf of San Blas (Atlantic side) and utilize a river approximately halfway across the Isthmus.
- In Colombia, the site is very close to the Panama border, and would use the Atrato and Truando Rivers to cross a land area of approximately 90 miles.

Thus far, most engineers favor the Caledonian route across the Isthmus of Darien, which would make use of existing water channels and require only a 30-mile cut. This would bring the canal out on the Pacific side near the site where Balboa got his first view of that ocean. Maritime experts favor a sea-level canal, thus eliminating the cumbersome locks which make passage so time-consuming and limit the size of the ships which can be accommodated.

The 110-foot width of the six, double (two-way) locks sharply limits the Panama Canal's capacity. A sea-level canal would have other advantages. It would be cheaper to operate, require less maintenance, and, if subject to atomic attack, could be put back into operation more readily than a lock canal. The plan is to use atomic power to blast a way through the isthmus. Dr. Gerald W. Johnson, assistant to the Secretary of Defense, declares that a canal can be dug with nuclear explosives at one-seventh the cost of conventional methods. His estimate is that a 1,000-foot-wide sea-level canal could be blasted across the isthmus for 750 million dollars. By comparison, he says that the cost of a 600-foot-wide canal using normal construction procedures would be more than five billion dollars.

No matter in what country the canal may be located, issues involving the purchase or rental of a new strip will occur. What will be the terms of sovereignty for the next canal? Who will own it, operate it, and fix tolls? If the new sea-level nuclear canal is constructed across the Isthmus of Darien in Panama, our political, military, and economic relationships with the Republic of Panama will be fundamentally altered. When and if the canal is dug, Panama will be certain to have its full say in how things are run. During the remainder of our tenure of the Panama Canal there will undoubtedly be gradual changes favoring Panama. But the Canal, as a Congressional committee has declared, "should not be permitted to become a pawn in our normal diplomatic relations with Panama."

Unless and until another canal is built, the Panama Canal will continue to be of great economic importance both to the United States and

Latin America. Any real erosion of our position in the Canal Zone is bound to have widespread and adverse effects throughout the Caribbean, in Latin America generally, and on our global relationships.

Professor Miller occupies the (Admiral) Milton E. Miles Chair of International Relations at the Naval War College, Newport, Rhode Island, where he has been teaching in the Naval Command Course since 1956. During World War II, he served with the Seventh Fleet as Air Combat Intelligence Officer and is currently a captain in the U.S. Naval Reserve. He has written on diplomatic and foreign affairs for leading periodicals and this is his fifth article for the *Proceedings*.

"Military Aspects of the Panama Canal Issue"

10

Lieutenant Colonel Jack Child, USA

U.S. Naval Institute *Proceedings*
(January 1980): 46–51

*Seventy-six years of American rule in the Canal Zone ended on
1 October 1979, when Panamanian Colonel Jose Contreras and
Lieutenant General Wallace H. Nutting, U.S. Army signed let-
ters recognizing Panamanian sovereignty in the area. We didn't,
however, relinquish our commitment to defend our interests in
the canal.*

DURING THE INTENSE congressional and national debate on the Panama Canal Treaties in 1977 and 1978, the military aspects of the canal
issue were a major consideration as arguments were presented assessing
its strategic significance. As the United States and Panama move into the
implementation phase of the 1977 treaties, it is clear that their military
provisions will continue to be important and will require attention and
understanding.

The Panama Canal was built when the battleship was the major strategic weapon and when being a great power necessarily implied being
a naval power. In this maritime vision, the centers of world power and
commerce were seen as linked by vital sea lines of communication which

passed through a series of choke points. Those nations able and willing to dominate the fairly small number of key choke points would be in a position to project their power efficiently. For the United States, a transoceanic canal in Central America was vital. With long coastlines on two oceans, as well as the Caribbean, the United States required a "two-ocean navy" to project its power. However, if naval forces and logistical resources could be rapidly shifted from one ocean to the other at a time of crisis, then the United States could employ its power far more efficiently and, in effect, have its "two-ocean navy" at the greatly reduced cost of a "one-ocean navy." The Panama Canal and the adjoining zone were significant not only as a conduit for shifting resources from one ocean to the other, but also as a major military staging area from which power could be exercised efficiently anywhere in the Caribbean, which came to be known as a "U.S. Lake."

With the coming of President Franklin D. Roosevelt's "good neighbor policy" in 1933, the instruments of U.S. influence in the Caribbean shifted from the blatantly military to the more subtly diplomatic, economic, and cultural elements. The unilateral and interventionist "U.S. Lake" strategy was replaced by the multilateral "hemisphere defense" concept and the establishment of pragmatic special relationships with those Latin American nations of greatest significance to the United States. The military value of the Panama Canal has declined in recent years, because of several reasons:

- Naval mobility and sea lines of communication are less significant now than they were when the canal was built. The warship is no longer the basic strategic weapon, and alternate solutions such as railroads, trucking, and air transport systems can contribute to solving the problem of shifting resources, although at a greater cost in time and money than the canal.
- The canal is vulnerable today to a much broader range of threats than it was 60 years ago, threats ranging from nuclear weapons to guerrilla warfare and political pressures.

- Technologically, the canal is becoming increasingly obsolescent. Large aircraft carriers and tankers cannot use it, and it diminishes submarines' element of surprise because they must surface in order to transit it.

Despite this decline in military significance, the canal was used extensively to move naval forces, troops, and supplies during World War II, the Korean and Vietnam conflicts, and the Cuban Missile Crisis. The consensus among military analysts today appears to be that the United States could survive without the Panama Canal, but its loss would require substantially greater numbers of ships and amounts of fuel, manpower, and other resources in order to be able to defend U.S. national interests abroad.

An interesting exercise to determine the scope of the problem was performed by the Congressional Research Service of the Library of Congress in late 1977. Its study described three specific situations and general conclusions:

- Mobilization of a 52,000-marine amphibious force to land in Northern Europe and fight in a NATO–Warsaw Pact conflict. With the canal available, 45 days would be required to assemble the force and get it to its destination; without the canal, 60 days would be needed.
- Shipment of munitions and other military supplies to aid a U.S. ally in East Asia. Since most U.S. munitions are manufactured on the eastern seaboard and there is only one munitions port on the West Coast, the most efficient method of shipment is via the Panama Canal; without the canal, other means would have to be employed which would be more expensive and slower and which might require cooperation by other nations.
- Use of the canal as an advance support base for an aircraft carrier task force off the western coast of South America. Although the task force could be supported and resupplied from bases in

southern California, the use of an advanced support base in the canal area greatly reduces the number of supply aircraft and ships and the time involved.

At the same time, there are still arguments supporting the idea that the canal remains an important military asset. For one thing, the canal area contains important bases for coordinating U.S. military activities in Latin America (regional headquarters, administration of military assistance, communications nets). In addition, major facilities for training the Latin American military are located there. Also, maintaining control of the canal would deny its use and control by a potential adversary. Lastly, at a time when U.S. power seems to be in serious decline elsewhere, the canal has a profound psychological significance as a military symbol of U.S. power in an area of the world historically of interest to the United States.

Physical Aspects: Vulnerabilities and Threats. From a defense standpoint, the major feature of the Panama Canal is that it is not really a canal at all; a canal is an excavated waterway between two larger bodies of water, as is the sea-level Suez Canal. In contrast to Suez, the Panama Canal uses an ingenious system of gravity-fed locks to raise ships 85 feet above sea level to a man-made lake. Ships then cross the continental divide on the surface of this lake and drop 85 feet back down to sea level on the other side through another series of locks.

This arrangement immediately suggests the two principal vulnerabilities of the Panama Canal: the lock system and the dams which hold in the manmade lake. Both locks and dams are fixed, known, and relatively large point targets vulnerable to sabotage, demolition raids, or air attacks. During the 1977–1978 debates on just how vulnerable they are, a few treaty advocates argued that the proverbial "man with a grenade" could put the canal out of operation for up to two years. This assumes a complete rupture of the lock system, the Gatun Dam spillway, or a Madden Lake dam—which would permit Gatun or Madden Lake to drain completely. Even after repairs, the canal would be out of operation for at least two rainy seasons until the lake regained its normal operating level. However, this amount of damage would not be easy to achieve since the locks and dams are heavy, reinforced, and likely to be under close guard during times of crisis. Gatun Spillway is a reinforced earthen dam one half mile thick at the base. The 7-foot thick lock gates weigh between approximately 400 and 700 tons. The various control sites and power installations required for Canal operations are more sensitive, but they are also easier to guard.

A different type of vulnerability is evident in some of the long stretches of narrow cuts, such as the 8-mile Gaillard Cut. The steep walls of the cut are subject to frequent natural slides and are vulnerable to being blocked by man-made slides. The narrow channels could also be blocked by a sunken ship. These narrow channel areas, with their dense jungle growth, are ideal sites for sniping and harassing attacks on shipping.

Human beings contribute to the canal's vulnerability as well. The group of individuals most critical to the canal's operation is the small, elite body of canal pilots. Their intimidation or elimination would effectively suspend the canal's operations. The majority (about 8,000) of the canal's employees are not U.S. citizens. Without this majority, the canal could not function at capacity unless U.S. citizen replacements were brought in from abroad. There are, however, almost 34,000 U.S. citizens residing in numerous canal housing areas, including about 9,000 military personnel, 4,500 Canal Company employees, and 17,000 dependents. Unless these individuals could be evacuated or concentrated in a small number of easily defended areas, they could be subject to harassment or capture as hostages.

A broad spectrum of threats can exploit these vulnerabilities. However, contemporary debate has tended not to concentrate on nuclear or conventional threats, since there is no defense against a nuclear attack and a conventional attack seems highly unlikely. Thus, attention has been focused on the danger of guerrilla raids and riots. This internal threat would involve irregular warfare in the dense jungles of the canal, with either passive or active support from the people, government, and armed forces of the Republic of Panama. A related possibility is the so-called "intervention by consent" situation in which outside volunteers or advisors (most likely Cubans) would enter the conflict at the invitation of the Panamanian Government.

In the face of these threats, the consensus among U.S. military leaders is that effective canal defense would require heavy reinforcement by troops from the United States. If the violence were widespread, the canal would probably be closed to commercial shipping, and defensive efforts would concentrate on the more vulnerable targets with the limited purpose of preventing destruction or long-term damage. In a 1976 letter to Senator Dick Clark, the State Department, in coordination with the Defense Department and the Central Intelligence Agency, assessed the U.S. forces which would be needed to defend the canal (but not necessarily to keep it open) in four separate situations:

- Sporadic attacks against locks, dams and other key points
- A commando operation, several thousand strong, against these points as well as against U.S. civilians
- The same commando operation supported by the Panamanian National Guard
- An all-out attack by Panama supported by 10,000 Cuban and Latin
- American troops trained in guerrilla Warfare and using military equipment from Cuba.[1]

To the first of these possibilities the State Department replied that canal police, augmented as necessary by a U.S. Army infantry brigade, would be sufficient. The reply to the last possibility was that 100,000 men, or three divisions, might be required. There was no specific numerical answer for the second and third possibilities, although reinforcements from the United States would obviously be required. The State Department letter pointed out that these situations all involved a breakdown of United States-Panama relations and that they indicated the need for a cooperative defense effort. The State Department also concluded that in the event of hostilities with Panama, the United States could expect little help or sympathy from Rio Treaty or NATO allies.

The U.S. Military Presence: The principal U.S. military headquarters is the U.S. Southern Command (USSOUTHCOM), headed by an Army three-star general with a two-star Air Force general as his deputy. The major tactical unit is the 193rd Infantry Brigade, composed of three infantry battalions (one of which is mechanized), a special forces battalion, an aviation battalion (mainly helicopters), an artillery battery, and various supporting units. The Air Force unit is tailored to support the brigade, and normally includes a total of 19 aircraft: helicopters, observation aircraft, fighters, and transports. The Navy has no ships or combat units assigned (although there is a marine company), but does operate fueling and communications stations.

The mission of these forces, and of USSOUTHCOM as a whole, goes beyond the narrow objective of canal defense as provided by the 1903 treaty. In effect, USSOUTHCOM is the regional U.S. military headquarters for Latin America, and its responsibilities include training the Latin American military, administering the military assistance program, carrying out humanitarian missions such as search and rescue and relief in case of disaster, operating communications, meteorological services, navigation and oceanographic activities, geodetic survey and mapping, and tropical testing.

A 1976 congressional report concluded that the 9,000-man U.S. military presence in the canal area is both too large and too small for most of the anticipated contingencies. It was judged "too small" to protect the whole canal from sabotage, harassment or a conventional invasion force, and "too large" because it has the potential of creating problems in the United States-Panama relationship.[2] Any threat exceeding limited and sporadic attacks would require reinforcement from the continental United States, especially if Panama were hostile and the Panamanian National Guard were to join in.

The National Guard: The Panamanian National Guard is a combined police-military organization and is the only uniformed force in the republic. As such, it must devote a major part of its energies to routine police work and has therefore not concentrated on the classic military mission of operating against an outside invader. With a strength of about 8,000, the guard is almost as large as the U.S. military presence, but 75% of these individuals are, in fact, policemen. The rest are organized as light infantry with about 1,500 men in seven rifle companies and six platoons. Their most advanced weapons are armored cars; the guard has no artillery, missiles, or tanks. There is a 200-man naval force equipped with light patrol craft and an air force unit of roughly the same size, which has some 30 aircraft, mainly helicopters and light transports.

The capabilities of the guard are greater than seem apparent at first glance. They have received considerable training (much of it at U.S. installations) in counterinsurgency and riot control. As an integrated police-military force, they have close contact with the grass roots of Panamanian society, and make conscious efforts to strengthen these links through an extensive civic action program. The junior officers and sergeants in particular are professionally impressive and imbued with a strong sense of nationalism. Thus, although the guard's capability to defend the canal or the nation against a conventional invader may be limited, it is well prepared to maintain internal order and to counter riots, sabotage, or guerrilla activities. Because of this orientation, members of the guard also possess an impressive capability to play the role of guerrillas or saboteurs against the canal if they choose.

The Cooperative Military Arrangement: The treaties establish an overall framework under which operation and defense of the canal gradually pass from the United States to Panama over the remainder of this century.

Within this framework is included a complex and delicate set of provisions dealing with defense aspects which can best be labeled the "cooperative military arrangement." The fundamental concept is that the United States retains primary responsibility for defense until 1999, but this responsibility is to be shared with Panama on an increasing scale until the final transfer of responsibility is made at noon on 31 December 1999. After that date, the United States and Panama will continue jointly to guarantee a permanent "regime of neutrality," but with no U.S. military presence on Panamanian soil.

Central to the concept of increasing Panamanian defense responsibilities is the need to increase the guard's capability to handle these responsibilities. In congressional testimony, USSOUTHCOM Commander Lieutenant General Dennis McAullife outlined a series of steps the United States was prepared to take to enhance the guard, including expanded training, military cooperation, and a $50 million military sales program.

Critics of the treaties have questioned the feasibility and necessity of this cooperative military arrangement, and also the fact that there would be no on-the-ground U.S. military presence after 1999. During the negotiating process it became clear, however, that for reasons of politics, pride, and sovereignty, the Panamanians would not accept a treaty with provisions for U.S. presence; the choice then became to accept a cooperative military arrangement with no U.S. military presence after 1999 or not have a treaty. Despite these limitations, however, the United States retains the right to act, unilaterally if necessary, to protect the canal and maintain its neutrality. Acceptance of these provisions reflects the realization that the basic U.S. interest is in the *use* of the canal, not in its ownership. The military aspects of the treaties and supporting documents thus represent, within the limits of the politically possible, a carefully crafted attempt to make the transition as smooth as possible.

The Permanent Neutrality Treaty contains three articles which deal with the joint agreement to maintain indefinitely the "regime of neutrality," starting from 1 October 1979, the day the basic Panama Canal Treaty went into force six months after exchange of the instruments of ratification. There is considerable ambiguity in the concept of "maintaining the regime of neutrality" which was seized upon by treaty opponents as an example of the "flawed" or "fuzzy" nature of the agreements. The ambiguity was, however, a careful choice of words which delicately straddled the gap between the assurances the United States required and the imperatives of Panamanian pride and sovereignty. This ambiguity was the subject of the "understanding" issued by the White House on 14 October 1977 after the meeting between U.S. President Jimmy Carter and Panamanian government head Omar Torrijos. The understanding clarified the U.S. right to take unilateral action to protect the canal and the "head of the line" provision for U.S. naval vessels in time of emergency. The understanding carried the important proviso that these interpretations do not mean that the United States has the right to intervene internally in Panama.

The "Agreement in Implementation of Article IV of the Panama Canal Treaty" lays out in detail the conditions under which U.S. troops can remain and operate in sovereign Panamanian territory until 1999. The implementing agreement also establishes a joint committee which will coordinate administrative aspects of the cooperative military agreement. The agreement makes an important distinction between "defense sites," which are under absolute U.S. control, and "military areas of coordination" in which there are joint patrols with Panamanian external security and U.S. military use and control for communications, training, housing, and other purposes. The foreign military sales package is contained in a "Note Regarding Economic and Military Cooperation," in which the United States offers to guarantee loans of up to $50 million over a ten-year period for the purpose of purchasing defense articles and services, subject to congressional approval.

Prospects for the Future: The bilateral cooperative military arrangement is complex and involves delicate and sensitive issues which may prove troublesome in years to come. Past experience with status of forces agreements and the problem of having U.S. troops on another nation's sovereign territory indicate the strong possibility of differences in interpretation and implementation, particularly in matters that Panama may consider as a test of its sovereignty and the United States in turn may see as unreasonable harassment.

Because of the patchwork of geographic areas under U.S. and Panamanian control, there will be numerous opportunities for inadvertent or deliberate intrusion by Panamanian squatters or demonstrators into areas still under U.S. control. Their policing and forceful eviction, if required, has the potential for tension and violence. There will no longer be a U.S. Canal Zone Police Force to act as first line of defense in such situations, nor will there be a U.S.-controlled intelligence agency as an integral part of the Canal Commission to provide warning of such situations, as the Canal Zone Internal Security Office did in pre-treaty days.[3]

A further concern is the likelihood of pressures to shorten the time until Panama assumes full responsibility for defense and all U.S. military forces leave. Presumably, if the cooperative arrangement works well and the Panamanians demonstrate a rapidly increasing capability to operate and defend the canal, the United States might be prepared to make some accommodations in the schedule.

Under ideal conditions, the U.S. and Panamanian military forces will enter into this cooperative military arrangement in good faith and with a willingness to go beyond a strict interpretation of the treaties to smooth over the inevitable minor frictions and avoid confrontation. As of late 1979, there was considerable ground for optimism. But this spirit of cooperation may break down between 1979 and 1999 over unforeseen contingencies and unresolved issues.

Interestingly, a little explored alternative does exist which could avoid U.S.-Panamanian confrontation: the multilateral option. The concept of turning part or all of the defense and operation of the canal over to a group of nations or an international organization has surfaced from time to time, beginning with the proposal made by Peruvian leader Victor Raul Haya de la Torre in the 1920s. Understandably, the Panamanians would object to this concept on the grounds that it would impair their sovereignty, while the United States would probably oppose the idea because of the inefficiency inherent in multilateral approaches. However, this multilateral solution might provide a temporary face-saving and time-gaining compromise behind which bilateral Panama-United States negotiations could resolve the issues under contention with less pressure and publicity. The creation of an international military body to defend the canal (even if only symbolically) would probably also run into opposition from those Latin nations which have historically objected to the creation of Inter-American military forces.

The United States and the Republic of Panama have embarked upon a lengthy, bold, and imaginative transition process in which defense considerations loom large. Military aspects of the Panama Canal issue demanded much attention and sensitivity in the protracted negotiation and ratification process. The legitimate security concerns of both principal parties, as well as those of the canal's users, will continue to challenge the best efforts and good will of all concerned throughout the rest of this century and beyond.

Notes

1. 94th Congress, 1st and 2nd sessions, Senate, Committee on Foreign Relations, *Panama Canal Treaty Hearings,* Part 1, 1977–78, pp. 180–83.
2. 94th Congress, 2nd session, House of Representatives, Committee on International Relations, *A New Canal Treaty: A Latin American Imperative* (U.S. Government Printing Office, 1976), p. 13.
3. Norman M. Smith, "Our Changing Role in Panama: An Overview," *Parameters,* September 1978, p. 15.

Lieutenant Colonel Child was commissioned in 1960 and from 1973 to 1978 served as Joint Chiefs of Staff Military Secretary to the U.S. delegation to the Inter-American Defense Board, the Joint

Brazil-United States Defense Commission, and the Joint Mexico-United States Defense Commission. He holds a B.A. degree from Yale University, an M.A. from the American University, and a Ph.D. in international studies (Latin America), also from the American University. He has taught Spanish at West Point and at the University of Maryland Extension Division in Saigon. Currently, Colonel Child is a faculty member of the Inter-American Defense College.

"Defending Panama"

11

Lieutenant Lawrence T. Peter, USN

U.S. Naval Institute *Proceedings*
(June 1990): 64–67

THE 20 DECEMBER 1989 U.S. invasion of Panama, Operation Just Cause, was a clear success for the United States. But Panama's stability is by no means assured; defense of the Panama Canal is at least as important now as at any time since the Carter-Torrijos treaties of 1977.

These treaties called for the development of Panamanian capability to defend the Canal after U.S. turnover in the year 2000, and guaranteed the permanent right of the United States to protect the Canal against aggression.

The U.S. Army's Corps of Engineers' assumption in February 1907 of the building of the Panama Canal led, in great part, to the Army becoming the primary government agency charged with ensuring the security and defense of the Canal. This relationship has remained in effect for more than 75 years; it may be partially responsible for Operation Just Cause.

Ever since Panama's independence (3 November 1903), the constant in terms of law enforcement has been the presence of the U.S. military; particularly the Army. Since 1977, U.S. Army efforts to implement the treaties resulted in the development of the Panamanian Defense Forces as an increasingly capable organization, more highly trained than its predecessor, the National Guard. The U.S. Army, the service that was principally responsible for developing Panama's ability to defend the Canal, designed a force that would have eventually included four battalions— one located at each end of the Canal and one at each border.

By Operation Just Cause's D-Day, there were more than 5,000 Panamanian troops, not counting paramilitaries; a small air element composed of a few helicopters, transports, and fewer than 1,500 personnel; and a naval element, the smallest of the three branches, with a few patrol craft and approximately 400 personnel.

It might seem strange that a country with a 50.2-mile-long canal, about 1,500 miles of coastline, and hundreds of islands would have a relatively small, incapable maritime force. But the primary role model for Panamanian armed forces was the U.S. Army, which actively pursued the development of a strong ground force. General Manuel Noriega used this force as the foundation for his regime, and ultimately, ironically, the U.S. Army (with assistance from the Navy and Air Force) tore it down.

What would Panama have been like if the U.S. Navy had provided that role model? Would the same thing have happened?

Since the U.S. Army always enjoyed a cooperative relationship with the Panamanian military, it is not surprising that our ally's force architecture mirrored it. Speculations aside about whether this was engineered in order to justify a continued U.S. military presence, the necessity to defend the Panama Canal was real.

And, though there may not be an obvious military threat to the Canal, this necessity still exists today. On Panama's western border lies Costa Rica, which has no army; it was outlawed in the 1940s. A threat to the Canal from a country without a military, more than 250 miles from the Canal, does not seem likely. Panama shares its eastern border with Colombia; the countries are separated by the virtually impenetrable Darien jungle, which has prevented even the completion of the Inter-American highway. The remaining threat axis would be waterborne, from Panama's Atlantic (northern) coast, or Pacific (southern) coast. While the country's

U.S. Army-style battalions might have been suitable to defend against amphibious landings, what Western Hemisphere country would have attempted such an assault, given the mutual interest in the Canal's continued operation?

The Canal is an asset of immense importance to international commerce, as well as to the U.S. military. In addition to treaty requirements calling for a Panamanian defense of the Canal, there is a very real need for an organization that can fill national defense-type needs. The type of Panamanian organization created will now undoubtedly be very different from the one envisioned by previous military assistance planners. The fledgling Panamanian government of President Guillermo Endara was quick to pledge that there would never be another Panamanian military. The need for one seems remote now, if indeed it ever was necessary.

The type of threat that faces the Canal requires a force endowed with the authority to enforce the law; this does not have to be a military organization.

The Threat: The Canal could be closed in a number of ways. They can be grouped, broadly, as follows; strategic threats, regional threats, terrorism, the threat from within (a regime gaining control and holding the Canal hostage; the "Noriega scenario"), and a general dilapidation of the physical plant.

- Today's strategic threat to the Panama Canal is vastly different from that before World War II, or in the first few decades after it. The current range of sophisticated land- and submarine-based strategic and tactical missiles, long-range bombers, and nuclear weapons would render the Canal virtually indefensible in a strategic conflict. Certainly the Canal could not be protected from such a threat by 3,000, 10,000, or even 25,000 troops.
- The regional threat appears as remote now as at any time in the Canal's history. Regional countries depend on the Panama Canal to varying degrees; this interdependence ensures its security.

- Terrorism, the threat of choice in the 1980s (and probably the 1990s), currently offers the greatest danger to the Panama Canal. It would likely be an act of retaliation and could involve threats or hostile acts such as a rocket- propelled grenade into the side of a liquefied petroleum gas tanker in the Culebra Cut or the surreptitious placement of mines by a roll-on roll-off ship in transit.

Currently, the best defense against terrorism is a highly refined intelligence collection plan that focuses on long-term indications and warning of possible events. The United States and allies are increasingly capable in this arena, and have shown a willingness to act against perpetrators when sufficient intelligence is available. However, terrorism's global nature makes it nearly impossible for a small country with limited resources, such as Panama, to staff a refined intelligence-collection plan adequately. In this area, the U.S. ability to detect possible threats to the Canal would be key to disrupting the terrorists' plans at their initial stage. More immediate threats could be dealt with directly between the U.S. and Panamanian governments. If necessary, the United States could ultimately invoke the permanent right of unilateral defense of the Canal and take whatever action was needed.

- The Noriega scenario could repeat itself if U.S. planners do not adequately safeguard democracy's future in Panama. Another threat from within could find Panama mired in an internecine conflict similar to those in El Salvador, Nicaragua, and Colombia. These threats are the most insidious; they tend to develop gradually. Without decisive corrective action, such as Operation Just Cause, too often the result is a regime with interests inimical to those of the United States and to democratic institutions worldwide.
- Less dramatic, but of equal concern, is the threat to the Canal from lack of maintenance or from get-rich-quick artists who

would use it for their own profit. While this is hard to prevent, the key to ensuring canal viability after U.S. withdrawal is to help all Panamanians feel that they own the Canal. During the next ten years, U.S. planners must redouble their efforts to ensure broad Panamanian participation in the Canal's future. Otherwise, a "Canal class" could emerge, that would grow fat off the riches of nepotism and cronyism. The result would be a Canal on the verge of collapse.

The Panamanian Maritime Force: Clearly, what is needed in Panama, not only to meet the U.S. treaty commitments but also to provide an organization capable of meeting the needs of a country that so strongly depends on maritime commerce, is a maritime force. A capable maritime force would provide Panama with a means to help ensure the safety of international shipping; it would also provide Panamanians with a national service with a logical link to their greatest inheritance—the Canal.

A force structure would have to be developed; two small squadrons of patrol craft, one on each coast, might be suitable. Typical craft of the maritime force could include Swiftships, both 105-foot and 65-foot fast patrol craft, as are currently in Costa Rica's maritime force inventory. Craft of this type would be ideally suited to a coastal patrol mission on both coasts. These maritime force patrol craft would provide a valuable service that would include:

- Search-and-rescue support to pleasure craft, fishermen, and commerce
- Drug-smuggling interdiction
- Disaster relief
- Maintenance of Canal buoys and other assets
- Regular humanitarian assistance to rural coastline villages

There is one additional benefit from a maritime force that would directly benefit Canal operations in future years. By treaty, all positions in the Panama Canal Commission are to be filled by Panamanians by the year 2000. In general, "Panamanization" of the Canal work force of 7,000 is proceeding quite well. Today, more than 85% of the permanent Canal work force is Panamanian (as opposed to less than two-thirds at the treaty signing in 1977). This is largely because of a successful Panama Canal Commission training program. But in some areas, Panamanization is not proceeding as well, and the U.S. Navy could help. It could provide expanded training opportunities for future enlisted personnel and officers in the maritime force, with billets at various training commands, A-schools, NROTC, and the Naval Academy. Skills learned would not only help build the new maritime patrol force, but also help develop essential Canal skills. For example, in the critical area of Panama Canal pilots, less than one-quarter of the approximately 240 current pilots are Panamanian. It is unrealistic to believe that the remainder of the Canal pilot force will be Panamanized by the year 2000. (Of course, alternatives could include contracting an independent pilot force.)

A proper U.S. Navy-developed maritime force could ultimately act as part of the feeder system for new Panama Canal pilots. Although the training pipeline to become an unrestricted licensed Canal pilot takes nearly ten years, seamanship learned through service in the Panamanian maritime force could provide the initial training for many new pilots. By the end of the next quarter century, Panamanians could be filling many, if not most of the piloting positions on the Canal. The benefit to the navies and merchant fleets of the world would be a highly proficient Panama Canal pilot force; one that would be capable of maintaining the high-caliber ship handling that the Panama Canal has been known for, and that would remain in place after the U.S. presence has ended.

For Panama, the benefits of a maritime force would include expanded career opportunities, a sense of ownership in the Canal's future, an adjunct to Canal operations, and a uniformed service that the country could be proud of.

Lieutenant Peter is currently assigned to Fleet Ocean Surveillance Information Center Europe under the Commander in Chief, U.S. Naval Forces, Europe, in London. He was the Panama analyst for U.S. Southern Command, Quarry Heights, Panama, from 1985 to 1989.

12 "A Panama Canal for a New Century: Wider, Speedier, Busier"

Commander Robert W. Selle, USNR (Ret.)

U.S. Naval Institute *Proceedings*
(September 2008): 30–31

THE U.S. NAVY'S LAUDABLE DECISION to stand up the Fourth Fleet (for the second time) on 1 July 2008 is welcome news for all those who believe in the progress and benefits of globalization and especially the role our Navy will play in the coming years in hemispheric and international relations.

Another element of transcendent relevance is Panama's October 2006 decision to complete the long-delayed Third Locks Project for the Panama Canal (originally begun in 1939 and halted during World War II). Work formally began in September 2007. When finished (expected by 2014), the Third Locks Project—with an initial cost estimate of $5.6 billion—will consist of a straight line course between just two lock sets, and it will allow passage of container ships carrying two-and-a-half times more cargo/containers, greater capacities, and shorter, safe, transits.

The construction plans are all state-of-the-art and include larger locks: 180 feet vs. 100 feet wide, 1,400 feet vs. 1,000 feet long, and 49 feet vs. 39 feet deep. In addition, the water level will be raised one-and-a-half feet by strengthening the Gatun Dam, and a new, straight, deeper channel will be dredged across Gatun Lake connecting the two lock sets.

One element of the new locks must be ascertained immediately. Can the *Nimitz-* and *Ford*-class carriers transit the canal safely? While the dimensions of both carriers are approximately the same (length 1,092 feet and beam 134 feet), will the lock width of 180 feet be adequate to accommodate the outward flair of the ship's side rising to 254 feet, the width of the flight deck? The rise and fall of the water level in each new lock chamber will be approximately 52 feet (the rise and fall of each new three-lock set will be approximately 155 feet total), and a problem of side fitting/scraping may arise when a *Nimitz-* or *Ford*-class carrier rises or falls over approximately 52 feet in any new lock chamber. But the depth of the chambers appears to be acceptable for safe passage.

Each lockset will consist of three lock chambers with the lock gates disappearing perpendicularly into the chamber walls—a big improvement over the swinging gates. In addition, control towers between locksets are eliminated as well as the present electric mules. All transit control will be accomplished by three maneuverable and powerful tugboats that use the highly efficient hydro-cycloidal Voith propulsion design technology. The essential watershed area surrounding Lake Madden will also be enlarged extensively and protected from all slash and burn devastation. Water use for the project estimates a savings of more than 60 percent over the present system, clearly a compelling projection.

Most certainly these welcome developments provide a quantum leap forward for political, economic, military, environmental, ecological, and humanitarian advances, both near- and long-term.

A Magnificent Sight

The absolutely thrilling sight awaiting us all is to see our largest carriers transit the Panama Canal. What magnificence and how stirring to all, particularly those of us in the Western Hemisphere! It is an acknowledged fact that transit of the Panama Canal makes two military ships out of one. Think of the time, fuel, and mileage saved—approximately

14,000 miles rounding Cape Horn—not to mention the reduction in wear and tear on the ship's company, machinery, and aircraft. We need a greater presence in the far Western and North Pacific areas, including the international waters of the strategically important Sea of Okhotsk, to counter Russia's and China's presence in the region.

We must include in our present analysis of events in the canal area the following:

- A thorough and complete study of the two original handover treaties, both the civil/political and the military. This analysis must develop all our rights and obligations thereto, and our study must be done in a friendly, non-confrontational, and coopera-tive manner.

- As to the construction costs of the Third Locks Project of $5.6 billion, we should consider that figure low and offer to pay for the entire project, even at double that estimate. It's worth it to us to ensure that the new locks can accommodate the *Nimitz*- and *Ford*-class carriers, not to mention civilian vessels such as Royal Caribbean's new *Oasis of the Seas*. If the Panamanians agree to our help, it would then be appropriate for the United States to participate in bond issues, in whole or in part, for construction costs and later for operational/maintenance costs. If done equi-tably and honestly, such costs could be beneficial to all interested parties and users.

- Upon Panamanian consent, the welcome return of the U.S. mil-itary presence would be an invitation to Fourth Fleet planners at all levels to enhance its already stated missions. Concurrently the U.S. Army, Air Force, Coast Guard, Public Health Service, Department of Justice, etc., under a similar agreement, could return to the area and reestablish the former Coast Guard sta-tion and the former Rodman Air Base with its large landing strip. The Jungle Warfare School, so prized by many Central and South American countries, could also be reestablished.

- Other activities helpful and beneficial to the area could include a permanent and expanded presence of our hospital ships operating in both oceans as well as a major health facility at Rodman field addressing combined tropical and general health issues. Such teaching facilities could be funded—as well as those on our hospital ships—by hospitals in the countries of the region.

The exciting plans awaiting Panama and Central and South America are directly in the center of the Fourth Fleet's operational area and are a positive extension of its mission. Most certainly these developments are visible on the horizon already. How and in what ways will the United States be proactive in understanding them? The 21st century requires *jointness* at all levels of planning and action. It is devoutly hoped that we will stand up and seize this historic moment!

Commander Selle is a member of the U.S. Naval Academy class of 1949. He served 17 years in the Office of Naval Intelligence (ONI) in various assignments.

INDEX

SERIES EDITOR

THOMAS J. CUTLER has been serving the U.S. Navy in various capacities for more than fifty years. The author of many articles and books, including several editions of *The Bluejacket's Manual* and *A Sailor's History of the U.S. Navy,* he is currently the director of professional publishing at the Naval Institute Press and Fleet Professor of Strategy and Policy with the Naval War College. He has received the William P. Clements Award for Excellence in Education as military teacher of the year at the U.S. Naval Academy, the Alfred Thayer Mahan Award for Naval Literature, the U.S. Maritime Literature Award, the Naval Institute Press Author of the Year Award, and the Commodore Dudley Knox Lifetime Achievement Award in Naval History.